The Revd Fraser Hancock
who was Incumbent
of St Lukes Church, Cheltenham
for seventeen years,
with many good wishes
from the Author;
H. White, 1889

Yours Obediently
H. White

Waite & Pettitt, Photos — Cheltenham

THE RECORD OF MY LIFE:

AN AUTOBIOGRAPHY

BY

HENRY WHITE.

Parvum parva decent.

CHELTENHAM:
Published by the Author,
BAGENDON HOUSE, ST. LUKE'S ROAD,
1889.
——o——
PRICE: THREE SHILLINGS.

PREFACE.

Ladies and Gentlemen,

You know me, White, the Bird-Stuffer? Well, a few years ago, an Idea suddenly flew into my head-workshop much to the disturbance of the customary work carried on therein; and notwithstanding several efforts on my part to get rid of my visitor, it continued to flutter about, raising clouds of dust and cobweb, the accumulations of many years, and thus disclosed upon the shelves numerous events, experiences, and things which had been placed there in the course of time, as and when done with, and which were almost forgotten.

As it was impossible to dispel the Idea, and equally so to resume ordinary work whilst the fuss and noise its presence created lasted, the only thing to be done, was to capture and kill it; so seizing it I was about to destroy it entirely, when I discovered it to be one of the family of "memoirs." It is scarcely necessary to state that these birds are somewhat rare, but they differ from *rara aves* as a rule in that their numbers are more likely to increase than to decrease as time goes on, until perhaps the place of the family skeleton will be usurped by the family memoir, both being remembered in future and better ages for having been remarkably *thin*.

My "memoir" struck me as being a curiosity, and I therefore preserved and exhibited it as such (free of charge) to a few friends at a social gathering in the Clare Street Mission Room, when they were kind enough to say it was also worth mounting, casing, and otherwise embellishing, after which I might boldly show it to a larger body of persons than were then and there assembled.

Acting upon their suggestion, I have since then devoted my leisure hours to the mounting and casing, and am at last able to present it to you completed; but I have found it necessary to make a small charge to defray the expenses of the present exhibition, the payment of which I hope you will never regret.

In pointing out that there are many birds of the same species already exhibited by others, which far excel mine in every quality, I beg to say that I do not claim that my "memoir" is anything but a poor specimen, dull of plumage and perchance malformed; but the fact of its being mine seemed sufficiently curious in itself to interest kindly all those who know me, though if I am wrong in this fancy, and the bird must be judged upon its merits, permit me to remind you that here, as in my museum, Visitors are respectfully requested not to touch the object—*roughly*

I am, Ladies and Gentlemen,
    Yours obediently,
       H. W.

Bagendon House, Cheltenham,
 January, 1889.

⁎ I wish to express my thanks to Mr. W. Lloyd Ferguson for the very humorous drawings with which he has kindly furnished this book.

CONTENTS.

AUTHOR'S PORTRAIT . . FRONTISPIECE.	
PREFACE	PAGE
I.—My Birth and Parentage . . .	5
II.—Youthful Days	13
III.—"College Life"	21
IV.—Work	25
V.—Farewell to Home . . .	54
VI.—My Second Situation . . .	68
VII.—A Taste of Forest Life . .	77
VIII.—Another Taste of Home . .	99
IX.—My Arrival in Cheltenham . .	105
X.—Married	118
XI.—Man's Worst Enemy is Man . .	134
XII.—Sunny Days	167
XIII.—A Bad Speculation . . .	172
XIV.—Final	178

ILLUSTRATIONS.

	PAGE
I.—Bagendon Church . . .	4
II.—Nearly Drowned . . .	20
III.—The Boy's First Occupation . .	36
IV.—Happy be thy Dreams . .	52
V.—The Boy in the Ploughfield . .	68
VI.—First Appearance in Livery . .	84
VII.—A Specimen of the Boy's Comic Work .	100

Badgendon Church.

CHAPTER I.

My Birth and Parentage.

ON the Twelfth day of June, 1822, I, HENRY WHITE, was born at Bagendon, a small village about thirteen miles from Cheltenham, and three and a half from the ancient and historic town of Cirencester.

I am consequently reminded that I am not a young man; but, were I asked how I feel with regard to the approach of old age, I should, without vanity, quote Dryden and say:—

> "He seem'd in years, yet in his years were seen
> A vernal vigour and autumnal green."

In fact, I feel as though I were not more than thirty years old. I am quite free from all physical pains, and not too stiff to climb a tree.

To use an every-day expression, I was born of "poor but honest" parents, my father being a country labourer and known in the village as the "useful man," his occupations being hedging, ditching, reaping, mowing and sowing; land-measuring for the farmers far and near; and groom, valet, coachman and general attendant to the village parson. He is also parish-clerk (having received that appointment in 1822, the year of my birth), sexton, bell-ringer, pew-opener, and grave-digger; and to add to his other accomplishments, he for many years presided at the church organ, the music of one "Handel" being played by means of another, the organ being of the old-fashioned "barrel" description. This instrument is now in my possession, and I invite any of my readers who may feel so inclined to call and try its powers. The organ will now, as in the days of yore emit in harmonious tones the good old tunes — "Old Hundredth," " Evening Hymn," " Sun of my Soul," " While Shepherds Watch," and many others which were used in those days when all could and did join in the musical services of the church.

To continue, however, as to my dear father's various occupations, whatever was wanted by any one, "William White" was applied to (William being my father's Christian name), and he was letter-writer to all in the village, shoe-maker and tailor, and was also known as the "village barber," besides being chief constable of the parish. His blue staff of office with a pair of hand-cuffs now hang in my museum,—relics of the past!

In speaking of my father and his many callings, what delight and pleasure thrill me at this stage of my journey! On sitting at the table with him, recently, enjoying a rural dinner in the cot where I was born, and looking at his grey hairs, his stooping form, his eyes grown dim, but rejoicing as he does in the possession of an unclouded mind, I could only hope and pray that having attained the ripe old age of ninety-six, he might be spared to become a centenarian. He has lived in the same cot for seventy-three years, and he has lived to see the many persons who resided in the village when he first went there, pass one by one to "the land beyond the skies!"

Now I would respectfully crave the indulgence of my readers for a moment, just to say a little of my mother. Yes, mother! If the name of "Father" is sweet, what is it to be able to say "Mother," especially to those who have had a loving one, as I had? I feel I cannot say enough of her, for she was all that was good. Alas! I can only speak of her, as she has long since passed away to her rest, and is now lying in the little village churchyard! But as I go on through the many twistings and turnings of my life, I shall have to speak of her again, and also of my father; for what I am penning down would not be complete without it.

Our family consisted of six boys and four girls, I being the third boy and fourth child, and we were all born in the same cottage. This cottage is over a hundred years old, and is one of an old-fashioned cluster of five, which were built more with a view to internal comfort than external beauty, and yet to a lover of the picturesque there is something very pleasing in these straggling, bulging, rough old houses, with their thatched and over-hanging roofs, as they stand surrounded by trees and shrubs, and gardens, "where many a garden-flower grows wild." Unfortunately, it has been decided to demolish them, and erect in their place others better suited to modern tastes and wants; but it is a grateful thought to me that out of respect for my aged father's wishes, the present owner has kindly consented to let these cottages remain untouched so long as my father lives, that he may peacably end therein a life which has flourished and waned in the same old home.

Having given a brief account of my parents and home, I will commence my own life, which has been a very checquered one.

A few details may not prove uninteresting to an indulgent public, and I will therefore go back to the day I was four years old. I may be asked how I can remember that. My answer is short—'tis simply, "Very well," and for this reason—in those days it was customary in our village for small boys, as well as girls, to wear petticoats, as knickerbockers were not known there, and on my *fourth* birthday my first pair of trousers made their appearance. My father, as I said before, being somewhat of a tailor, had managed to make them. I don't remember the kind of material they were made of; I know it was not West of England broadcloth; but I well remember the colour—it was a sort of yellow, something similar to nankeen. There was a great deal of talk at home and among my playmates, for some weeks previous to the day they were to be put on, as to how they would look, and so forth. At length the eventful day arrived, the 12th of June, 1826, after a very indifferent night's rest for me, which had been broken by light airy dreams of the yellowish nankeen, and I believe each member of the family took a part in the performance of donning them. Father and mother were there, brothers and sisters were there, and, of course, your humble servant was there, all looking for the trousers. However, be that as it may, Henry managed to put them on, and there he was, there he stood, first looking at one leg, then at the other, arrayed, I dare say, in as curious and gorgeous a pair of trousers as ever excited the envy of a child's juniors and the laughter of his seniors. My father gave me a two-penny knife for one pocket, and my mother a penny for the other; and the first time I went down the village street the boys and girls cried out, "Oh! there goes Harry White, with his yellow trousers!" and I can safely say that from that day until now I have never appeared in any kind of female attire.

CHAPTER II.

Youthful Days.

I will now draw the curtain over a period of two years of my young life, nothing of any importance having occurred; all I had to do was to eat, sleep and grow.

Well do I remember those early days of my boyhood, when all seemed to go smoothly along with the running stream; no care, no sorrow of any kind to mar the pleasures of the day, or to interfere with the innocent amusements enjoyed, as a rule, by children of that tender age; living, as it were, only for the day, like many of our beautiful butterflies—sporting in the sunshine only for a few hours;—happy, happy child; no care, no thought for the morrow.

Being now six years old, my parents thought it high time to send me to school, (although they had themselves taught me my letters, so that I was quite capable of repeating the alphabet correctly), and I was accordingly sent to one kept by a dear old woman, and I remained there under her primitive tuition for about two years. This old lady had but one leg, I remember, and the boys would frequently take advantage of the fact, but she always kept by her side a long hazel stick, measuring six or seven feet in length, so that when brought into requisition she could manage to reach either of us without getting up from her chair. How often did the boys take hold of the end of the stick and pull it from her hand, thinking it rare fun! I remember very well committing the act once myself, but I felt it was wrong and regretted it ever afterwards. I managed pretty well to keep in her good graces by doing little acts of kindness for her every now and then, by watering her flowers, making a fire, peeling potatoes, running to the village shop for tea, butter, sugar or eggs, for which I often received a halfpenny, and young as I was, I held the high post of first teacher in the school, having to hear the lessons of the other children. What a position for a curly headed boy seven years old!

I continued with her, as I have said, until I was eight years of age, and, having made the best use of my time, I could read pretty well. My parents now thought I could be of use to them at home; as there were several younger brothers and sisters requiring attention, my dear mother felt she must have some assistance in the nursery department, being about all day. So, after a little consultation, it was decided for me to take the situation of under-nurse, an elder brother being placed over me, which I certainly did not like. This went on for about two years, when my elder brother left home, and as I had conducted myself properly and in a competent manner during that time, I was promoted to the position of head-nurse. My duties were confined to managing a younger brother and sister, and in preparing the meals by the time my parents returned home. Dinner had to be ready by twelve o'clock, and I am proud to say I always had it so prepared. Even then the seeds of punctuality had been sown, and were beginning to bear fruit. Well do I remember a quotation of my father's,

which has never been lost upon me :—
"Punctuality, honesty, and perseverance will carry a man through anything." I must admit that I did not always excel as a cook, as the following incident will testify. My dear mother was very particular about potatoes being cooked well, as she considered it was the most important dish brought to table, and one day it chanced that the children were very tiresome, especially my little sister, something seemed wrong with her, and having to give her extra attention I was a little behind-hand with the dinner. Fearing my parents would be home before it was ready, I made up a little extra fire to boil the potatoes quickly, but, unfortunately, I allowed them to stay a few minutes too long, for, to my horror, I found they had boiled to a pulp. Upon my parents coming in, I stated the case to my mother, laying the blame on the baby, and saying

how cross she had been all the morning, and what trouble I had had with her; but I omitted to say I had given her a good shake, which I really had. My parents, however, satisfactorily accounted for the crying, by saying baby was cutting another tooth, and so, under the circumstances, I was not scolded for my mishap. Another of my domestic failures here comes vividly back to me. Having on a certain day to procure water for tea-drinking purposes, I rocked the two children to sleep, and then took my pitcher to the brook, a stream of water running through the village, where all could draw from it. Small and narrow was the stream, as it peacefully murmured its way through the village, affording sport to the children, who delighted to chase the tiny minnow as it darted to its mossy home amid the bubbling waters. Soon, however, did the little rivulet join a greater, and so proceed in gathering strength until it was finally lost in the waters of the mighty Thames. Now, close to the old cot, a shallow well had been formed at a particular bend in the stream, where, with bucket or pitcher, water might be more readily obtained, the stream itself not being of sufficient depth, and on stooping down for my supply, my foot slipped, and in I went, head foremost, and I suppose found the bottom, for when I was brought to land I had more mud upon me than when I went down. How long I might have remained in that element I cannot say, but luckily for me one Richard Cole, a man of the village, rescued me and placed me on the stone I had fallen from a few minutes before, where I stood very wet and dirty, and cold, and miserable, but beyond this, and feeling very frightened, I was none the worse for my "dip." A good, motherly neighbour, who came on the scene soon lent a helping hand, and put me in fair trim again, saying "the boy was all right." I then thought it was time to see about the children, so, finding my way into the nursery, I was pleased to find their peaceful slumbers had not been disturbed by their nurse falling overboard. On the arrival of my father and mother the case was soon made known to them, and they took care afterwards to have the water ready for me. Thus ended my first and last experience in deep sea fishing; and I thankfully record the fact that but for my timely rescue by good Richard Cole (who has long since passed away), my life's history would, at a very early period, have had "finis" written upon its pages.

Nearly Drowned.

CHAPTER III.

"College Life."

HAVING now attained my ninth year, my parents held a consultation as to the practicability of again sending me to school; not to a poor unfortunate woman with only one leg, but to a good schoolmaster who could boast of two. Accordingly a tutor was found, named Dix, at Duntesbourne, a village distant about four miles from my home. Arrangements were soon made for me to go, and on a particular Monday morning I took my departure for the new school. Unfortunately there were no railways, and I had consequently to tramp the four miles morning and night. This, even to a boy, was no idle matter, especially in the winter, and many times on my return at night has my dear father come to meet me on the way, in case I should get lost in the snow. The winters in those days, I need hardly say, were more severe than now; often did the frost continue for seven and eight weeks at a time, the snow being between three and four feet deep, and frequently have I seen the farmers' men digging out the sheep from under it. I soon made friends with my new companions, and not more than a week elapsed before I felt quite at home with every one. I took so active a part in their various sports and games that I was soon looked upon as their "captain": whatever was going on I had to be consulted, whenever a grievance arose I had to act as umpire—so that it is not too much to say that a hearty spirit of good fellowship was quickly established between us.

A schoolboy's life does not, as a rule, embrace events of sufficient importance to place on record. Work and holidays, lessons and play, rain and sunshine, year in and year out, these were the sum and substance of my two years' stay at this new school, and it is even now pleasing to remember that I received but one caning, for playing during lessons, which, however, made me feel as though I had been walking in a sugar plantation of great extent. I had now made tolerable progress in my studies; true I had only one tutor, who taught me the three R's, but having no grammar or French masters to contend with, I was the better enabled to perfect myself in an education which was likely to prove all-sufficient in my after life. At the end of two years I was obliged to say farewell, not without a tear of sorrow, for I had made many friends, and the regrets at my leaving were many and sincere. Mr. Dix himself was good enough to add his testimony as to my general good conduct during the time I had been his pupil, and to reward me with a prize, and an excellent character.

CHAPTER IV.

Work.

NOW having reached the mature age of ten years, and my parents having to provide for the daily wants of several other little ones, I had to prepare to take my part in bearing the burden and heat of the day. It was about harvest-time, the middle of August, 1832, when I commenced to toil for my daily bread. A farmer of the village wanted a boy to act as crow-keeper—by no means an intellectual occupation, but at least a useful one—and my father applied for and obtained the post for me. I have said "crow-keeper," but it should rather be "crow-disperser," my duty being to frighten away, by shouting and springing a large rattle, the crows and rooks that consumed the corn without so much as an "if you please."

For the first few days I felt very sad and lonely; I thought much of being away from home so long, as my hours were from seven in the morning until six in the evening, and many days often passed without my exchanging a word with any one. It was then that my thoughts wandered back to my school-days and the many bright scenes associated with that happy period. However, I made the best of my work, monotonous as it was, for I knew that in the satisfactory performance of it my duty lay. For some time I was at a loss to know when the dinner hour had arrived, or how the day was speeding, for I seldom saw anyone to ask, but an idea struck me that something might be learned by the sun. The farmer coming to pay me a visit on the day that I was thus cogitating, I ventured to ask him the time, blushing as I did so. He informed me that it was just twelve o'clock, so, taking my stand in a line with a large ash tree, I noticed in what direction and how far my shadow fell at that hour. By this simple expedient I was ever afterwards able to tell, by a clock which never failed, the time of dinner, and by thus converting myself into a sun-dial, subsequently learned the hours of three and five o'clock.

It was here, while dispersing the birds, I first imbibed a taste for natural history. I well remember a certain day, sitting in a stone-quarry eating my dinner, which consisted of bread and cheese. As I sat, a large beetle emerged from the grass and crawled up my trousers—*not* the nankeen ones,—and as he crawled he seemed to say, " Can you spare me a crumb ? " I at once supplied him with a little, willingly sharing what I had with him. I then set to work to build him a kind of house, the materials being small stones and dirt; the latter I mixed with water, which was near at hand, and formed a kind of mortar or cement. In this house I kept my beetle for several days, seeming as it did quite content with the homely fare I could place before it, and very well it thrived under the new conditions of life. This beetle, its habits and peculiarities, formed the foundation of my love for natural history, a love I have cherished and cultivated until now.

Having now spent about three weeks attending and making friends (?) with the crows and rooks, I had to wish them good-bye, for the time had come for the reapers to thrust in their sickles—the corn had ripened and my services could be dispensed with. During the time I had been employed I had been counting upon my first earnings, and upon pay-day arriving the farmer asked my father "how much he expected per day for the boy?" My father said, "Well, Sir; I think he is worth sixpence at any rate, young as he is." "Oh, dear no," said my employer, "nothing of the kind; I shall only give him threepence." Now, fancy a young fellow working for nearly twelve hours for that sum: seventy-two hours a week for one shilling and sixpence! Small as the sum was, however, I knew it would be very acceptable to my persevering father and mother, who were toiling early and late to supply our wants; and the munificent payment was accordingly accepted. Harvest having now commenced in all directions, my father and mother taking part in it, it was soon settled for me to go with them, knowing I could be useful in drawing the bands of wheat and tying up the sheaves. With sickle across my shoulder, I therefore, reaper-like, wended my way to the field of wheat for the first time, and at once commenced my new duties. In about an hour I had become quite an adept in the art of drawing bands, and so satisfied was my father with the work that he did not hesitate to place the sickle in my hand by way of experiment to test my abilities. This I also very soon mastered, to the astonishment of all my neighbours, who were eyeing every movement of the new recruit. I remember one very hot day I was working away with all my might, and was just in the act of drawing the sickle round a handful of corn, when I made a mistake, drawing it round my finger instead, and cutting it very badly indeed, and the mark I bear to this day as a memento of the past. Having worked in the harvest-field until all was gathered in, I next engaged in turnip hoeing, under the superintendence of my father, and so well did I execute the work that my pay was raised to sixpence per day. After I had been thus employed for about a fortnight, the farmer informed me he should require me for a more important post in a few days, namely, that of pig-keeping in a neighbouring village, the practice being at the close of the harvest to turn the pigs into the fields to pick up the loose ears of corn. I cannot say I cared for this occupation, for it was very monotonous. On a certain day, however, an incident occurred which I cannot help recalling. Being somewhat tired, I sat down beneath a shady tree, and, rendered drowsy by the heat, I fell asleep. How long I slept I cannot say, but, judging from the sun and my feelings of hunger on awakening, I felt sure it must be near my dinner hour. As my sheltered seat formed an excellent dining place, I turned for my dinner bag, which I had deposited near me on falling asleep, and as I looked my attention was attracted by the grunting of one of the old pigs. He was vigorously shaking a piece of linen which he held in his mouth, and on going to the animal I found to my horror that it was my dinner bag, the strings having become entangled in his teeth. The contents of the bag had all disappeared—whether he had shared them among his fellows I cannot say, but not a crumb was to be found, and I was without a dinner. I am not quite sure what the bill-of-fare was on that particular day, but to the best of my recollection my careful and attentive mother, in addition to bread and cheese, had put in my bag a baked apple-dumpling by way of a "second course." Hunger could now hold out no longer, so "borrowing" two turnips from the adjoining field, and a few blackberries by way of dessert, with a draught of pure water from a spring close at hand, I made a tolerably good dinner, and on the next day my bag might have been seen hanging from a tree, and, as you may suppose, out of reach of the old pig.

At the expiration of three weeks, I was removed from the stubble-field to the plough-field, there to drive plough (or rather horses), instead of pigs, a very different occupation from either of my former ones. I soon acquired the familiar cries of "gee-up," "come-ethor," and "go-on-Jollie." My new work tired me greatly, and many times I was privileged to ride home in the evening, on the barebacked horses, my feet resting on the traces for stirrups. In a few weeks, I had acquired sufficient knowledge of horses to take charge of the whole team, and so proud did I feel at boasting another accomplishment, that I really thought I was entitled to the degree of M.A. I would here note, that I was not one of the strongest of boys, my parents had always considered me the most delicate of the family, often saying I was "more like a girl." I continued with the horses until the middle of October, getting on very well with them, but as winter was coming, my father thought it would not be wise for me to continue with them through the cold weather, and he accordingly took me away. I cannot say I was sorry to leave, for I found ploughing and tilling the land very laborious work, and after walking over the clods of earth all day, my feet were so blistered at night I often cried to have my boots taken off.

I did not remain idle very long, for my father had arranged that I should join him in his usual winter's work, hedging, cutting and laying hedges, this being usually done at the fall of the leaf. I therefore joined my father in this new business, as co-partner, or rather, White and Son,—this was certainly rising a step higher, slow, but sure. I commenced the first day in right good earnest as you may suppose, everything was again new to me, but in a few days I seemed quite master of the hatchet and bill-hook, and in a few weeks was able to make a faggot. It was the very severe winter of 1832,—as my father can testify, for only a few weeks ago when sitting at home with him on his ninety-fifth birthday, he said we have not had such a severe winter since,—and I suffered acutely from the intense cold, although my hands were thrust into thick buck-skin gloves, proof against thorns, and my legs encased in leather buskins. By way of keeping the blood in circulation, I often had a run across the field and back, and every day I lit a fire about eleven o'clock, the dead wood from the hedges serving as fuel. I always managed to have a good fire by dinner time, and this was very comfortable to dine by. Having, in my early days at home, as my readers are already aware, acquired some little knowledge of cooking, especially potatoes, I was able to make a great addition to our dinner by baking some in the wood ashes, a mode of cooking that I even now enjoy and can thoroughly recommend.

The winter, long and severe as it was, finally came like all other things, to a close, and spring was with us, the trees with renewed vigour putting forth their green buds, flowers appearing in every nook and corner, the glorious sun bursting through the dark clouds which had hid it so long, the beautiful birds warbling forth their songs of love, making all nature joyous, and everything teeming

The Boy's First Occupation.

with life around us. "What a change then does nature present, from the cold dreary winter, on the opening of lovely spring. Everyone must have experienced the joyous feelings awakened by the first burst of song, 'the time of singing birds,' as Scripture so beautifully describes it. Were the eyes to refuse their office, those notes that ring on the ear would call up before the imagination gleams of warm yet passing sunshine, leafless trees wearing a purple hue from the tint of their bursting buds, the fresh green grass, the daffodils and violets, and all the accompaniments of the new-born spring. It is not, however, in the spring only that their notes call up so many associations; when their song is silent in the summer, still the air resounds with the calls of the old birds to their young, and we could scarcely fancy it Autumn, even if we saw the leaves changing and the rime upon the ground, if we did not hear the "cawing" of the rook breaking the calm stillness of the morning, and when we return home in the close of the winter's day, and all the birds are hastening like ourselves to the night's shelter, should we not miss the robin's little parting song, and scarcely believe it evening, because we did not hear it."*

Now, being so much employed in the fields at early morn and late at eve the notes of birds thus became very familiar to me, and were associated with the scenes around me. I took a pleasure in observing their habits, and found them subjects of continual interest. When the long winter has passed, and we ourselves or those around us have been suffering from its changes—its cold one day and its damp the next—how welcome are the first tokens of returning spring. We begin to venture out in the early hours of the morning. At

---
* Life of Charles Waterton, Naturalist.

first we catch a glimpse of the beautiful little wheatear on the common; the next morning we hear the chiff-chaff repeating his usual monotonous note, in the usual place, as if he had never been away; then the little willow wren begins his merry song like a hearty laugh, telling us the perils of his journey are over, and he is safe; the black cap follows, with his clear and beautiful notes, till at last we listen with joyous and almost breathless attention to the first note of the thrice welcome cuckoo. And what a strange influence have these two notes gained over us: spring to us could not be spring without them. Some years ago, I think it was in the year 1835, the cuckoo was unusually late—April passed, and yet no one had heard the cuckoo; a kind of vague, uncomfortable superstition was creeping over the minds of the rural population, and they began to think some vast change was at hand. A friend informed me that he was in the early part of the month of May of that year, accompanying a friend in a walk to some labourers engaged in draining, and while they were there, the cuckoo flew over their heads, singing his long-expected song. The men threw down their spades, and exclaimed, as with a feeling of relief, " He is come at last!" How often did I myself make the same remark to my father, "Oh! there's the cuckoo!" When, indeed, we look at the little birds of passage hopping among the branches, with their slender bodies and feeble wings, they seem to awaken all those feelings of interest and respect which it is the privilege of great travellers to inspire. The imagination wanders to the sunny climes that they have been visiting, the strange and distant scenes among which they have been sojourning, the perils they have encountered, and the wonderful instinct that has brought them back. Those little wings have borne them over lands which it may never in all probability be our lot to visit, and those puny travellers have penetrated into countries beyond our reach. Their return calls up to our imagination scenes of distant beauty of which we have read. What strange accounts could they give us of what they had seen in the mysterious depths of Africa—its stately palms, its desert fountains, vast plains, and herds. There is a mystery connected with their wanderings which increases the interest with which we witness their return. Birds are of such an active nature, their forms generally so beautiful, and all their energies so strongly developed, that they all become prominent features in the scenes where we find them, and thus become strongly associated with their localities. Thus, in visiting the Zoological Gardens, the power of the associations they excite must have been often experienced by those, fond of observing. When we see the heron standing half asleep, after his morning meal, how quickly does the mind travel to the distant mountain stream, where I have often seen him standing, of which he and the water-owsel were the only inhabitants. I have often seen the heron standing on one leg in the middle of as tream, the neck thrown out, and the head reposing on the shoulders as it were when, all of a sudden, down went the long beak into the water, and with one jerk of the head bring out a large fish, oftentimes from ten to fifteen inches long. They are also particularly fond of the water newts. It is a most interesting sight to watch them. Why should we not endeavour to connect these objects of interest, so continually inviting our observation, with more useful associations than those of distant scenes and past days. It were better for us that they should speak to us, if we can make them do so, rather of the future than the past. Why may we not try to scatter a few words of warning and instruction along this path of daily observation, as we hear of some zealous persons scattering tracts in the turnpike road, content with the satisfactory conclusion that if one in a thousand take effect they shall be well repaid. In the spring of the year, the period of which I am now writing, the birds seemed to forcibly attract my attention, and to excite my interest. It was at such times as these that the love for natural history seemed to force itself upon me; it was then, in the woods and fields, where I had such chances, of making many observations, and becoming acquainted with my feathered friends. In the month of April how busy and energetic they all are. Having chosen their mate, then comes the important question as to the site of the nest and the supply of materials for forming it. The grass is now beginning to grow, and the temperature to increase, and the cattle and the horses are throwing off their winter coats. It is now that the Almighty Creator of the Heavens and the Earth, who hath called all things into existence at a word, and can multiply to infinity the works of His hands, teaches us a lesson of carefulness, and warns us that He hath made nothing to be wasted. As the cattle cast their coats, the birds come in for their share; we see the daw, and the starling, and others hastening to the spots where the cattle have been lying, to appropriate the cast-off hair for the lining of their nests. We should endeavour to follow in the spiritual, an example so beautifully displayed in the natural world, and strive to connect earthly with heavenly objects, that nothing may be lost. Here I must stop, and ask a pardon for leaving the high road for the green fields; but the old haunts and scenes of my early days are still so vivid to the memory, that I seem to be travelling back again from whence I started, and my pen knows no bounds.

To my tale. I went on working with my father for three years, work varying with time, and in accordance with the seasons. My hours at this time being the same as my father's, my evenings were generally spent in football, hockey, rounders, or hare and hounds, in all of which I joined with the other lads of the village. I well remember a little, and I may say an amusing, incident which occurred at that time. It was a very hot summer, consequently wasps were very numerous. It was considered rare fun with the boys to take a wasps' nest. On meeting with one in a hollow tree in the wood, it was decided we should take it. My brother George, with Job Belcher, an old school companion, and myself, made up the party. Accordingly we set off, having furnished ourselves with the proper requisites for the taking of the nest. On nearing the spot we soon commenced the business; my two companions, however, felt alarmed when they saw the little creatures so busy. I called them cowards; Job Belcher replied, saying, "Well, I don't want to get stung," so bracing up my nerves I forced away a piece of the decayed wood, exposing the nest, when out rushed the wasps by scores. I at once made my exit at some speed, but unfortunately I fell down, being entirely surrounded by the wasps, and my two assistants laughing at me. However, with their assistance and my own exertions, we dispersed them, but not until I had had several thrusts from their pointed daggers, my head and neck having suffered severely. I looked upon the incident as a stinging recollection.

I continued working with my father until I attained the age of fifteen. After my day's work had concluded, I generally spent half-an-hour in perfecting myself in writing and arithmetic, so that I should not forget what I had learnt at school. I was then allowed one hour for recreation, which I spent, as previously stated, with my "college" companions. One little incident, connected with my father, I must not omit here. I remember one day we were felling trees at the village of Daglingworth, one mile from our home. We expected every minute to see the tree fall, and as it began to crack, which was a signal for us to get out of the way, my father cried out, "Run, Henry." Well, I did run, and so did my father, but one of the uppermost branches struck him across the back of his neck, knocking him down. Oh! I shall ever remember seeing him lying there—as I thought, dead. He was carried to a farmhouse, where every attention was paid him, and a medical man was soon in attendance, who pronounced him not seriously injured. Later on in the evening he was conveyed home, and, with good nursing, was able in a few days to resume his work, but he felt the effect of the blow for several months.

My father and mother at this period often held consultations as to my future life, for being of opinion that I was not one of the strongest of boys, they thought that an indoor occupation of some description would better suit me. With this view, my father mentioned the matter to our friend the farmer, thinking he would be a likely person to help me. He at once promised to do what he could for me, and in a few days he informed us he had seen a gentleman who was in want of a lad about my own age, to live in the house, attend table, clean boots and knives, do a little gardening, and make himself generally useful; also to look after an "Arabian Mule," better known as a donkey, which I had to attend as groom and coachman, having to drive him into the town of Cirencester once or twice a week for the purpose of shopping. The farmer said he had mentioned my name to the gentleman, and had made a favourable report as to my character and abilities. In a day or two an order came for my father to take me for inspection by the gentleman, who resided at the little village of Duntesbourne, three miles distant from my own home. It was the worthy Rector of that place, the Rev. Dr. Sisson. Accordingly my father took me, and how well do I remember the Doctor saying, " I like the appearance of the boy very much." Turning to me, he said, " Do you think you would like to wear livery clothes, boy?" Of course I answered in the affirmative, and an arrangement was made for me to go a month upon trial. The Doctor was quite satisfied with what the farmer had said as to my character, etc., and then came the question of wages. Now he did not ask what my terms were, but explained his own, which were rather low. The first year I was to have two pounds, — the whole of forty shillings!—and my clothes as well. My father made a remark as to the sum being small, but the Doctor said, "Oh, but I shall have to show him everything; coming from the plough-field he will be quite ignorant of all indoor work." On hearing that remark I felt my cheeks glow with indignation for I remembered the dif-different offices I had filled with success; I felt quite indignant with him, but I don't think he discovered it. Well, my father consented for me to take the situation upon those terms, and to go the following

Monday. Here, then, was another change before me, which was to be the final one. In a few more days I should have to leave home, father and mother, brothers and sisters, and all my old companions; the word "good-bye" would have to be spoken, and then the great separation. Now, whether it was for joy at the thoughts of going, or sorrow for leaving, I cannot say, but several hours passed away that night before I could settle comfortably in my hammock, but towards the morning I fell asleep, and was soon dreaming of the black plush breeches, white stockings, and low shoes, with buckles, that I was to wear in my new employ.

Now, one more incident occurred before I left home, which I must mention before closing this chapter. On the last Sunday previous to the day I was to take my departure, my brother Fred induced me to have a game of marbles, being the last evening we should be together. Unfortunately for us, both consented. Now I knew and felt it was wrong to do so, to disobey my father's orders. However, we played the game, and I came off captain, winning the stakes. Fred, feeling annoyed at his loss, picked the marbles up, and putting them all in his pocket, ran away. Of course, boy-like, I followed him, giving him a push, which caused him to fall, cutting his forehead very badly. My father coming out just at the minute, seeing the blood streaming down his face, very naturally enquired the cause. I told him. His only remark was, "Oh! so you have been playing again on a Sunday, have you? Now come in-doors, I want to show you something." Ah, that something; there was the look, and the same hazel-stick reached down from where it had been resting for some time; then came the usual order "Take off your jackets," when about the same num-

ber of strokes were administered as on the last occasion, but this time we were allowed supper, being my last evening. I saw a tear trickle down my dear mother's cheek as she said, "William, don't beat the boys; it is the last time they will play together; Henry is going away in the morning." My father replied by saying, "No matter; I have forbid them all playing on a Sunday." Her petition in our favour that time had no weight with him. I shall never forget my feelings on that ever memorable evening: my heart seemed breaking, and I believe my dear father felt each blow quite as much as we did ourselves, but it served us right, he only did his duty, for he was always loving and kind. Here, then, on my last evening at home, sitting in the old chimney corner, I will close this chapter.

CHAPTER V.

Farewell to Home.

HERE commences the great chapter of my life. For fifteen years had I been moving onwards, travelling at a moderate speed, and without getting my fleece torn, or receiving the prick of a thorn, but I was now to experience some of the many ills of life that reach us all. The day arrived when I was to say "good-bye" to all, and to seek a new home. I will not attempt to describe my feelings on that eventful morning, for they were beyond description, as will be readily imagined by my readers. For several days previous had my dear and careful mother been unusually busy, preparing my outfit and setting all in order. Everything being packed up in a neat box, I was prepared for a start, but as I sat down to my last breakfast I felt I could not do justice to it, for my heart seemed breaking, especially when I saw the tears trickling down my dear mother's face. That was a trying hour, both for mother and boy, and how vividly does it occur to me even now at this advanced stage of my life. The moment arrived for the last fond kiss to be given, so, with a hearty and warm grasp of the hand and a shower of kisses, I said good-bye to my loving mother, and brothers and sisters. My wardrobe and other personal belongings were not at that period very numerous, and so were easily divided between my father and myself, he carrying my box and I slinging a bundle upon my shoulder. Thus did I, Dick Whittington like, save that the cat was missing, take a last look at, and turn my back upon, my dear old home. Fifty-one years have rolled by since that eventful morning—being then in my fifteenth year,—and how little did I then think of the many thorns that would bestrew my path where I looked for the flowers to grow. Ah, is it not well for us that we are unable to dive into the future? Little did I then think of the many hard battles I should have to fight before reaching the end of my life's journey. Methinks I can see father and son wending their way across the fields towards their destination, the boy paying attention to the good advice and counsel of his parent. Oh! I seem to remember every step that we took side by side until we reached the Rectory, which was to be my new home. On arriving there, which we did a little before ten o'clock, I was ushered into the presence of the Doctor, to undergo an inspection by him and his wife and daughter. Closely was I scrutinised by each and all, and it was with the most profound feeling of satisfaction that I heard my inspectors at the close of their examination, say, "We think he will suit us very well." I then left the august presence of the Doctor, for the purpose of making certain final arrangements with my father. The dear old man then put five shillings in my hand, saying, "This is your fortune; it is all I can give you, but when you are in want of more, write and let me know. Take also my blessing, and may God guide you. In your box you will find a small parcel from your mother; pay attention to what it contains." I was not long in turning out my box to see what was in the parcel. On opening it I found my bible, very carefully wrapped up, which I had had given me by the clergyman of the parish when I was eleven years of age, and I rejoice to say it is still in my possession. Having partaken of the Doctor's hospitality, my father bade me good-bye, and I was left among strangers to make my way in quite a different sphere of life to that which I had hitherto been accustomed to. Having been shown through the house, and having inspected the out-buildings, the Doctor subsequently called me to go with him, saying he wanted to show me the pig-stye and stable. I concluded at once I should have to make the acquaintance of swine again, and my surmise was correct, for there were three, which I had to feed regularly. On entering the stable I expected to see one or two horses, instead of which there was a donkey. It appeared I was to act both as coachman and groom, for the

Doctor remarked to me, " As you have been accustomed to horses I suppose you can manage this Arabian." At the end of a week I was pretty well versed in the general routine of my various occupations, and I was happy to learn that my employers thought I should suit very well. By this time I began to feel at home with everyone, and my various duties seemed to come quite natural to me. The order was then given that on the following Monday I was to go to Cirencester to get measured for the talked-of livery, which was to be ready the following Saturday. The day arrived, and so did the clothes, and I shall never forget my feelings on donning my new attire. First came the low, shining shoes, white stockings, black plush breeches, with bright buckle and buttons at the knees, a brilliant brimstone-coloured waistcoat, covered by a bright sky-blue coat, pigeon-tailed, of course, with a stand-up collar, embroidered with two rows of gold braid, and finishing with a set of bright yellow buttons. This was a harlequin dress indeed, and at this period I can only liken it to the costume worn by some of the attendants at a well-to-do circus. My next ordeal was to undergo an inspection once more in the drawing-room. The verdict was again satisfactory, but I can well remember that my young mistress was pleased to make some allusion to the smallness of my legs, but this, as the Doctor sagely remarked, was an evil which would grow less every day. The worst part of my experience in this magpie livery had yet to come, for I was to appear in it the next day at church. Now the Rectory house was close to the churchyard, having only to pass through a side door. In the morning my order was to be ready five minutes before eleven, full dressed. As the seeds of punctuality had already been sown in me, I was ready to the time, standing by the side door waiting for the family to pass through. They soon made their appearance, the Doctor asking me to carry his church surplice on my arm; this I had to do every Sunday. The family having all passed through, I was ordered to fall in in the rear, and as soon as we entered the churchyard there was a general uproar among the boys and girls of the village, who had assembled to get a sight of the new footman. By some means they had found out that he was to put in his appearance at church that day, and I shall never forget the running fire of good-natured banter that I had to undergo as I wended my way to the church door. The worst feature in it was that I could not in any way resent it, but I confess my blood was at boiling point, and willingly would I have exchanged my position for that of driving the plough or pigs, in fact anything would have been preferable to my then situation. As soon as I had deposited the surplice in the clergyman's pew,—in lieu of the vestry, there not being one,—I was shown to my seat, a kind of faculty one, belonging to the Rectory. I had not been long in it before I could see I was the observed of all observers. Every eye was upon me, or at any rate seemed to be, and the congregation appeared to take more interest in the new comer than they did in the service. The sermon was only about fifteen minutes long, but to me it seemed a good hour, and I think I am right in saying this was the most tiresome period of fifteen minutes I ever endured. Service over, I had to take up my position again, the order of things being reversed, and the same terrible ordeal had again to be gone through in the afternoon at the second service. This time, however, the task was less severe, and the remarks not being so many I fared somewhat better than in the morning. In about a fortnight I had made friends with many of the villagers, and was able to associate with them without being molested in any way, and as time went on the novelty of my attire wore off, greatly to my satisfaction. At the end of two months my master and mistress thought it high time I should begin to learn the art of waiting at table, and it was therefore arranged for me to attend the next day as a few friends were coming to dinner. I was ordered to appear in full dress, of course acting under the orders of the parlourmaid, who was a most excellent waitress, and understood her duties in every branch. I assisted her in laying the cloth for the first time, and the Doctor coming into the room a few minutes before dinner gave the order for me to station myself in a corner of the room, and to remain there during dinner-time and not attempt to do anything. Now this was a great disappointment to me, for I had been counting upon doing something. Dinner-time was now near at hand, and the first guest arrived,—a gentleman who has since befriended me on several occasions. He asked, " Is Doctor Sisson at home ? " Of course I said, "Yes," but instead of showing him into the drawing-room I left him standing in the hall, where he was subsequently found by the parlour-maid. This, then, was my first blunder. Dinner being served, I took up my position in the place assigned to me, and there I stood like a statue, quite at a loss to know what I should do with myself; the order was to pay attention to my tutor. Now, the soup plates having been cleared away and the fish brought on, I thought I could easily do the same thing—merely pick up a dirty plate. Accordingly, the maid having left the room,

I watched my opportunity, and seeing my master had finished, I emerged from my corner, seized his plate, and was about to rush off with it, when he immediately called me back, bidding me put it down again and go back into my corner. This quite unnerved me, as my readers may suppose; and how little I seemed to look. I really did feel nervous, for I wanted to be doing something. However, I managed to remain quiet until the dinner was finished. This was my first attempt to do anything in a dining-room, but afterwards I assisted regularly every day, and soon became acquainted with the work. So I went on from day to day for a period of two years, during which time nothing of any particular note occurred. The Doctor now made an exchange of livings, and became Rector of Barnsley, a village distant about four miles from Cirencester. Here I remained about four months, when it was decided to make some different arrangements in the house, one being not to keep a man servant, and consequently I received the usual month's notice to leave. This was a great blow to me, for I confess I had been sailing along very comfortably. At the expiration of a week I heard a Mr. Newmarch, solicitor, of Cirencester, was in want of a man servant. I at once applied for the situation, and my credentials proving in every way satisfactory, I obtained the place. Thanks to my friend the parlour-maid, —who has since died,—from whom I had acquired much valuable information, which was likely to be of great assistance to me in my new situation. My month's notice having expired a little monetary transaction took place between me and the worthy Doctor, and I was ready for a start. I was not allowed to leave without receiving a present from him by way of compliment, and he said he should be glad to render me any assistance that lay in his power at any time, and with a hearty shake of the hand from each member of the family, and many good wishes for my future welfare, I once more said "good-bye."

CHAPTER VI.

My Second Situation.

AFTER leaving Barnsley I had a few days allowed me by way of a holiday, before going into my new situation, and I therefore made for home, dear old Bagendon. Having been away from it two years, all were pleased to see me again, and I was soon called upon by my former companions to join them in

The Boy in the Plough Field

some of the old games. Oh! what pleasure I experienced as I sat in the old chimney corner, again occupying the same stool I had used two years before on the Sunday evening previous to leaving home. How it all seems to cling to the memory, and with what force does it come back to me, painting each thought with bright colours of the past, and re-kindling the hopes and aspirations of a long ago. The week which had been given me flew quickly and pleasantly, for I passed most of the time wandering in the fields and woods where I had so frequently been. I seemed to recognise every moss-covered stick and fantastic stone that had attracted my attention in the days of old. Even now, when I pay an occasional visit to my dear old father, do I wander to the old stile under the wood, where I have often sat late in the evening alone, enjoying the solitary hour—nothing to disturb the attention, save the screech and whirring note of the night-jar, or the whooping of the brown owl, as these midnight marauders sally forth in quest of prey. Many times have I visited the same spot late at night, expressly to hear my friend the owl give one or two of his night calls, and seldom have I had to wait long before being greeted with the usual welcome, as much as to say, "I have been expecting you." I think of all birds the call of the owl is the grandest. There certainly is something very solemn and weird in its note, especially when the listener is sitting in a wood at ten or eleven o'clock at night alone, as I have often done. I was rather startled on one occasion by the appearance of a huge head, adorned with long horns, looking over the wall close by where I was sitting, at an angle in the wood. I felt a kind of chill creep over me, but only for a moment, for summoning up courage, I ventured to the

MY SECOND SITUATION. 71

place to ascertain the nature of my nocturnal visitor, when I discovered it was only one of the farmer's cows which had come to make friends with me. The incident was simple, but I never pass the wood without thinking of it.

The day now arrived for me to take my departure once more—two years older than when I said good-bye the first time, and certainly two inches taller, having attained my seventeenth year. Leaving all my old associations behind, I went on my way rejoicing to the town of Cirencester, where I had again to be introduced to new society. I found this, my second situation, somewhat different from the first, for I had a horse and carriage to look after which occupied the most of my time, but every day I attended dinner, filling up any odd hours in the garden. All went well for several months, when my master was ordered away into

Yorkshire for change of air, his health having been impaired by reason of a severe accident some two or three years previously. York was the place decided upon, the family having relations there; and as it was arranged for me to go also, I considered it a great treat to become such a traveller and to go so far away from home.

While staying at York I had fine opportunities of visiting the Cathedral, or I would say the Minster, with its fine organ, containing four-thousand, five-hundred pipes. This ancient city possesses many objects of interest, not the least attractive being the old city walls with their four principal entrances. During our stay of three months, I enjoyed myself exceedingly, for I was able, by rising about five in the morning, to explore the entire district, rich in antiquarian lore. I had always been an early riser, and am now, for I love the fresh and gentle breeze of the early morn, the sparkling dew drops hanging on every blade of grass, the shrill chirp of the grasshopper, and the sweet notes of the early birds. The hedge rows covered with the wild and creeping honey-suckle, and the scent from the well-known may-blossom all added to the enjoyment of the early walk; and then to crown it all there was the bright and glorious sun bursting forth over the hills in the far-off Eastern sky and making still more beautiful a scene already entrancing by the entire absence of the hum and bustle of the then sleeping world. At the end of the three months we returned home again, and I venture to say both master and man had benefitted by the change. During the three years I remained in this situation, nothing of any particular note occurred. I had now acquired a good general knowledge of my duties, and I consequently considered I was competent to take a better situation and receive higher wages. This matter I laid before my master and mistress who coincided with my views, but said that although they had no wish to make a change, they could not increase my salary, and I therefore gave them the usual month's notice. Before the time expired, I succeeded in obtaining another situation in the Forest of Dean, as under-butler, and was sent for to Gloucester to see my new master. We soon arranged matters, and having received a good character from Mr. Newmarch, my future employer did not hesitate in engaging me, and desired me to enter his service the day I left Mr. Newmarch. This did not quite agree with my feelings, for I thought I should like a few days again with dear father and mother and some of my associates, including the old owl; so I managed to get a week as I did on the previous occasion, three years before—once again did I say farewell—and on the evening of the same day I was to be seen as usual, seated in the old chimney corner. I spent this holiday as before, in visiting my old companions and schoolfellows and journeying to my old haunts. I did not forget to pay my nocturnal visit to the wood, and the first night I might have been seen comfortably seated on the old stile. In a few minutes I heard my friend the brown owl pouring forth his evening song, welcoming me back again after an absence of three years; once, twice, and thrice came the whoop from his musical throat as much as to say "Ah! what, come again?" I well remember its being a beautiful moonlight night, and I am compelled to give expression to the thought that of all seasons and times the still hour of night, away from all and alone, nothing visible but the bright moon and twinkling stars in the far-off Heavens, is the most enjoyable to the contemplative mind. The calm serenity of the evening tempted me to remain out of doors, but I was compelled to wish my hooting friend good night, or, rather, farewell, for I thought it highly probable we should not meet again for some time, telling him if I returned at some future period I would not forget him.

CHAPTER VII.

A Taste of Forest Life.

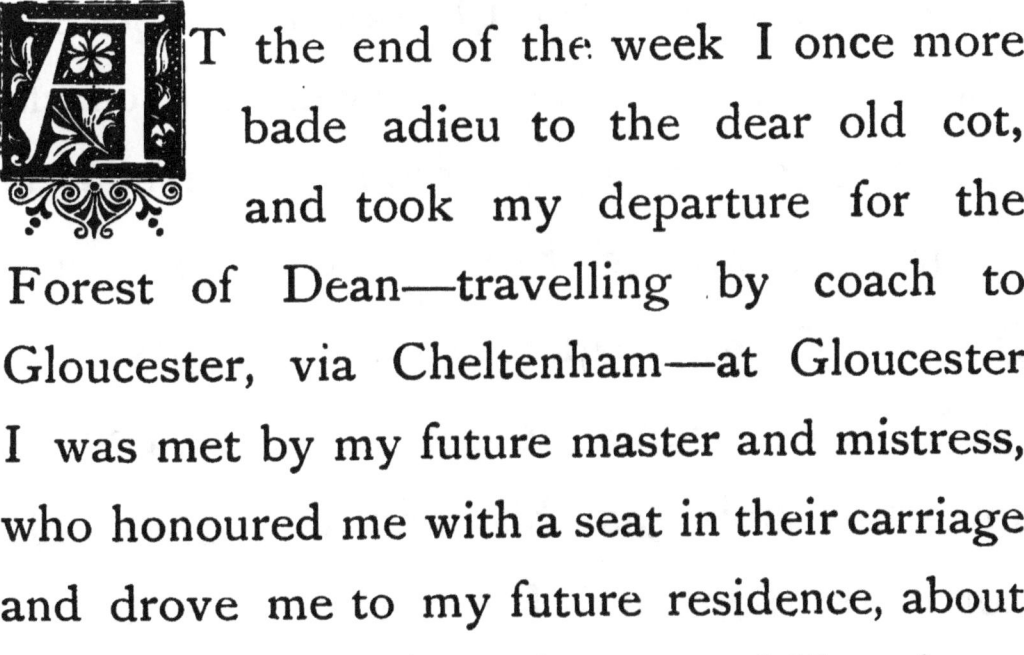

AT the end of the week I once more bade adieu to the dear old cot, and took my departure for the Forest of Dean—travelling by coach to Gloucester, via Cheltenham—at Gloucester I was met by my future master and mistress, who honoured me with a seat in their carriage and drove me to my future residence, about two miles distant from the town of Newnham.

Our route followed the course of the Severn nearly the whole way, and I had an opportunity of seeing the Kittiwake and other Sea-Gulls: my information relative to natural history had hitherto been confined to the lanes and woods of my native village, where birds of the briny ocean were seldom seen. I confess, I felt rather lonely the first night, being placed among strangers, and was glad to retire to rest; and endeavour by indulging in the many bright and cheerful scenes of the past to create hope and comfort for the future—thus occupied, I lay awake for several hours, but not so a fellow-servant, the coachman, who shared my bedroom; unfortunately for me, he proved to be a great snorer, and if any of my readers have ever passed a night with a companion who made such an unearthly noise as this man did, I am truly sorry for them and I feel sure they in turn would sympathise with me; I never heard such sounds proceed from any human being before, and to my sorrow and annoyance I had to endure this sound, making as it did, night hideous for three years. It was rather remarkable, but he generally commenced the horrible noise about twelve o'clock, and with his mouth open he presented anything but a pleasing spectacle. Utterly worn out, I at length fell asleep—sleep that was rendered pleasant by sweet dreams of home—but I was soon awakened by what I may term an extra snore, given in quite a different key from any of the previous ones, in fact it was so loud it actually awoke the sleeper himself. On mentioning the subject to him in the morning he expressed his surprise, replying in a cool sort of way, "Oh, that is nothing, you will soon get used to it." Singularly to say, in a few weeks I really did get accustomed to it, in fact I looked for it as regularly as the night came round, and indeed should have missed the sonorous lullaby that now hushed me to sleep. I soon made friends with all the servants, who were most agreeable in every way. My co partner the butler, was most particular with everything in the pantry,—the work had to be well-done, and done to time—all rules most strictly carried out, nothing was put aside for the morrow; I may say he was a little too severe with me, but his teaching benefitted me in after years, and to this day I have to thank him for what he set before me. To him I owe much of the knowledge I possess; he showed me everything he possibly could, in fact, he was as a second father to me, but like many more of my friends, he has been summoned to his rest; also the coachman, the house-keeper, two house-maids, the gardener, laundry-maid, the game-keeper, master, mistress, two sons, and the eldest daughter, all have gone. Oh, how much there is for the mind to dwell upon in those two little words rest and gone; the voices we once heard are now hushed, the still familiar faces are out of sight, and we can only bring them before us by summoning the sweet memories of the past. The youngest daughter of the family is still alive, and only a short time ago I had the great pleasure of accommodating her with a seat in St. Luke's Church, Cheltenham

The first summer passed and winter had set in, when the family began to give dinner. parties. Here again I had new opportunities of picking up fresh ideas; the good old butler ever ready to set me right when wrong; always ready to assist me when in any difficulty, so that by attention and perseverance, as time went on I gained experience. My master and mistress were particularly kind to me, as were all other members of the family, in fact I seemed to sail along splendidly—not a ripple on the waters to impede the progress of my boat in any way; all was bright and calm, so I went on month by month, nothing particular happening worth recording in these memoirs. An amusing incident, however, occurred one night the second winter I was there. The family had been dining out at Newnham, returning home about half-past eleven. It was a beautiful clear moonlight night, and as one of the horses had to be taken to a distant part of the estate, it was consigned to me to take it. I confess I felt a little timid, for it was a very lonely road, and at the bottom of the hill was a wood which I had to pass through. On getting into the middle the horse became very restive. I could not get him to move either way. His eyes seemed fixed on something in the distance; its mane and tail stood erect, and the more I pulled to get him on the more he pulled back. I quite thought I must let go my hold. I tried harsh means as well as coaxing, but it was all of no use; he now commenced snorting and pricking up his ears, still looking in the same direction. In a few minutes I distinctly saw some object myself, about thirty yards away among the trees, but could not discern what it was. My feelings may easily be imagined. Every hair on my head was, like the horse's mane, perpendicular; my coat seemed to move on my back, and my flesh felt frozen. After some few minutes I managed to get the horse on, but still had some distance to go through the wood. My charge appeared to be as much frightened as I was, but having eventually reached the field, and having removed the halter from the horse's neck, I bade him good night. Now the worst part had to come—having to return the same way—oh, horrors! I was in a strange place, not knowing the locality, and not being aware of any other road to take, I knew I must pass the same way again. So summoning up all the courage I could, I began to retrace my steps. On reaching the spot, which I had marked by a large tree, I made a stand and, although my knees were bending under me, I seemed to gain strength for the occasion, so venturing to look in the direction where I had previously seen the object, I soon satisfied myself it was still there and could distinctly see it move. However I went on as fast as ever my legs could take me, not caring to look behind me once. Glad I was on reaching the main road again. I have many times regretted that I did not go to see what caused the alarm. Had I done so, I fancy I should have found it was a stray cow or sheep from the adjoining field, but I here confess this was the only time in my life I was ever frightened. On reaching home and narrating the circumstance to my fellow-servants, I was only laughed at, as a matter of course, and whenever I think of it

First appearance in Livery before his Master and Mistress.

I certainly feel a little ashamed of my weakness. No doubt many people would have rushed home full of excitement, saying they had seen a ghost—a tall figure with bright eyes, dressed in white, as they generally are, but I refrained from drawing upon my imagination to this extent.

I have often heard that horses can at night distinguish objects more readily than any other known animal, but I sincerely wished on this occasion that my four-footed friend's vision had been limited, and so have given me no cause for alarm. No other adventure occurred worth noting until about twelve months afterwards, when I was taken ill with violent and constant pains in my head, being at times quite delirious. A Doctor Bird of Newnham, the family attendant, was called in, and he recommended cupping, which was done at once. I was branded for life, for in each of my shoulders may be seen the incisions then made by the cupping knife, twenty-four distinct white lines, twelve on each side. Rather "sharp to the eyes" was this operation, and it seemed to relieve me but little. The next remedy was to have a seton in the back of my neck, and no sooner said than done. This was much sharper than the cupping; and two white lines still mark the spot where the skein of silk was drawn through the flesh, where it remained for a month. This punished me a great deal, but certainly relieved me. I remained in a very weak state for several weeks, when the Doctor recommended my removal to the Infirmary at Gloucester, where I was at once taken. Here, then, was another change for the young man—placed among strangers again, new faces, new ways, new scenes, new everything. I shall never forget the first night of my new lodging, being the occupant of No. 5 Ward, where

A TASTE OF FOREST LIFE. 87

there were about twelve beds; and from the groans of some and the deep sighs of others I had but little sleep. It was there in the stillness of the night that my thoughts wandered away to distant scenes— dear old home, father, mother, brothers, and sisters all that was then dear to me. I soon found I was in the hands of a good nurse, and in a day or two had made friends with her, and was not long before I fell in with their everyday bill of fare, which was varied three times a week. I could not say much in favour of their made dishes, for the cooks were a long way behind in sending up savoury ones, especially on what we called bone days, which was every Wednesday. On this day we had a kind of soup, each patient getting a bone with it. I was lucky enough on two occasions during my stay to have a marrow bone. I cannot well give the soup a name, but I can say it was not ox tail nor mock turtle, it was more like thin gruel. Twice a week we had pudding, but often suet dumpling, and considered it rather aristocratic to get a "second course." For breakfast many of the inmates had porridge, others milk. I was highly favoured, being allowed tea, with bread and butter, which is a favourite breakfast with me, never caring for meat with the early meal. Having made friends with the nurse, I was a little favoured in many ways unknown to the other patients; there were many little tit-bits put by for me, from time to time, after the nurse's dinner. She was particularly fond of flowers, like myself, and I had to take the whole charge of them in the shape of watering and tending them, also sweeping and dusting her room, and in many other ways did I make myself useful to the good nurse. I also often assisted the other patients, who were not so convalescent as I was, in making their beds, as each one was expected to make his own, at least, those who were able. I always felt I could not do sufficient for the nurse, as she was so good and kind in every way — a noble-minded woman, possessing a kind and feeling heart and generous disposition; always a cheerful word for all around her; a pleasant look with a woman's sweet smile of love, which I always think helps one on so much through the day, let one's toil be never so hard, and I would say "bless them."

It was now drawing towards Shrove Tuesday, and having a weakness for pancakes, I felt determined I would have some if possible; I therefore called a hospital council meeting, and laid the matter before them. The meeting was to be held in the large ward, at ten in the morning. Summoning five of the young men about my own age, who at once voted in favour of the pancakes, the business was soon settled, signed, and sealed, but the question arose as to who should prepare them. The lot fell upon the writer. Now, although I had been cook some years before, I had never fried pancakes; however, I felt I could do it, and undertook at once the responsibility to see that all preparations were duly carried out. Before the meeting broke up I made a suggestion that the nurse should be consulted upon the matter, for I foresaw she would have to be referred to about the frying pan, and what was more important than all, the fire. She obeyed the summons at once; I was obliged to be spokesman, and having duly explained all particulars, relative to our meeting, she cordially gave her consent, both as to frying pan and fire. The first step was to obtain the materials for the work, for it was only a week to the time. Now what was to be done for flour: there were six hungry men to be provided for, and neither was very well of, as to cash; so we arranged the number of visitors should be limited: no one to sit down to the banquet but those who had contributed. Now twice a week we had, for dinner, what is known in the North, as *labscouse*, that is a very thick kind of gruel, made, I believe, from flour and water; well, the thought struck me if each one put by his portion, instead of eating it, this would do very well for batter. This question was therefore put to the meeting, and, of course, carried. The next item was lard, a most important ingredient in the affair, and I was again appealed to as to what to do; my reply was, to-morrow is bone day, pick the meat off, but save the bones. All seemed to approve of this plan, which was accordingly adopted on two occasions. The day before Shrove Tuesday I collected them together in a large bucket, took them down into the wood-house, and with a large hatchet borrowed from the carpenter, I chopped them in pieces; among them there were three marrow bones of which I took care, knowing the marrow would not be a bad substitute for lard. The next process was to boil them, one of my mates remarking, "But what about a saucepan?" The second one said, pointing to me, "Oh, leave that to Harry, he will manage it." That had been previously arranged with my good friend the nurse, so I very soon had them on the fire. As the fat boiled I carefully skimmed it off, putting it into a basin, and I was not long before I had what I thought would be sufficient to fry the pancakes with. This, then, was my substitute for lard. My sole thoughts that night were the pancakes; and even in my sleep I seemed to be busy mixing up the batter, and fancied I could see a huge pile on the dish, the steam covering me with a cloud of vapour. One of my companions, who was lying at some distance from me, called out as I was falling asleep, "Harry, don't forget the pancakes to-morrow, mind you make plenty, for I can manage four or five myself."

In the morning my companions were all astir before the usual time, and the leader came to my bedside and gave me a good shake, saying, "Get up, this is pancake day." I said, "Bother the pancakes—no rest I suppose until you have had them." As soon as we had breakfasted and all was cleared away, preparations were at once commenced; every one was busy doing something—like so many cooks in a kitchen. I calculated it would take about one hour and a quarter to fry the pancakes, so I soon gave the order to have the dishes of batter brought in which had been put aside from our dinners. I did not forget the milk, for I managed to get a quart with the consent of the nurse, the expense of that and one pound of sugar to be defrayed by us all.

The ingredients being ready, I turned the first cupful of batter into the frying pan, when, in about two minutes, instead of thickening as I expected, it all turned to water,—here was a disappointment! However I kept on frying, but the more I fried the thinner it became. All the fat coming to the top, of course it would not mix with my batter. I gave it a fair trial, but the marrow from the bones still floated on the top. I felt myself beaten and all my fond anticipations of the pancakes seemed gone. I quite thought I should have been able to have given lessons in cookery, or a new way of making pancakes, but I had failed altogether. I was cogitating as to the cause of my failure, when the thought struck me that I had omitted the eggs. Here was a blunder! However I kept on boiling, for I could'nt say frying, until I had finished it; turning the whole into a huge basin. We commenced eating, using spoons instead of forks; but I confess the taste of it was no more like pancakes than lobster sauce is like current jelly. Whenever I smell, see, or taste a pancake I am reminded of those I attempted to make in Gloucester Infirmary; but bad as it was, we gave the nurse a very polite invitation to join us. She just tasted the mixture, saying "How can you eat it?" So ends the story of the pancakes, which I never forgot.

After being in the Institution about a month, I began to mend and soon found my way into the garden, making friends with the gardener. I often helped him in his work, and while so engaged one day I attracted the attention of the House Surgeon. Calling me into his room, he very carefully examined me as to my state of health, when he didn't hesitate to pronounce me sufficiently recovered to have my discharge, which was accordingly given to me for the following Thursday. I must not omit to say a few words in favour of the noble institution, and would recommend persons needing them to avail themselves of its many privileges, for there the best medical advice is to be had, the best of nurses, with careful attention, combined with cleanliness. I cannot speak too highly of its merits. During the time I was there I made many friends, and certainly spent a very happy time, and to day I recognise the fact that a friendship formed in a few weeks often lingers in the memory for years. On quitting the Infirmary, the first persons to greet me were my master and mistress, who asked me where I was going, and on my replying that I intended returning home to see my parents, they insisted on my going with them as they wanted me back. All my plans and hopes were thus frustrated, and so does it ever seem to be when all appears clear before us, a cloud, albeit, no bigger than a man's hand, arises shutting out all that is bright and beautiful. Here then was another bitter disappointment, but there was no alternative but to yield to my master's wish; I, therefore, took my seat on the carriage and was very soon rattling along the road again by the side of the Severn. On reaching the old mansion in the Forest, all my fellow-servants were glad to see me, and no little rejoicing was manifested on my return, having been away five weeks. I felt myself very much better, and was able to resume my duties. Nearly three years had expired when my health failed the second time; Dr. Bird was accordingly consulted, when he at once said it would be much better for me to go home and have a few months' rest, and arrangements were accordingly made for me to leave forthwith. It was with considerable regret, that I parted with master and fellow-servants, for the one had shewn me no little kindness, and the others had proved genial and pleasant companions; necessity, however, which knows no law, compelled me once more to say farewell.—And accordingly, with a good certificate of discharge, and a hearty God speed from all, I bade adieu to the old Forest.

CHAPTER VIII.

Another Taste of Home.

THE morning I left the Forest my master conveyed me to Newnham, where I took coach for Gloucester, and presented myself at Bagendon, about five o'clock the same day, having apprised my parents some days previously of my coming home. On sitting at the table with my dear father and mother enjoying a high tea after my long ride, I recounted my little adventure in the wood with the horse; and then related the story of the pancakes, explaining the whole process as to how they were made.—My dear mother laughed until she cried, when I thought it was high time to cease, but I well remember her saying, "Oh, go on; tell us something more for I like to hear you talk."—Nothing loth, I recounted to my willing auditors all the most interesting incidents that had occurred to me by flood and field. I returned home to find our family group somewhat less than usual, four brothers and sisters having left home since my last visit, my youngest sister being the only one at home with my father and mother. This sister was the one I had charge of in my early days, at the time I was head nurse; many, many times have I rocked her to sleep in the home-made cradle, where I myself had laid and kicked, exerting my lungs to their fullest extent.

The First of September.
A Specimen of the Boys Comic Work.

After a good night's rest in my old hammock, where I had lain twenty years before, I rose early in the morning, as was my custom, and prepared breakfast, which seemed quite natural to me to do. My father giving a hint as to what was wanted to be done in the garden—he himself being busy elsewhere—I at once set to work in good earnest, although not very well, for I never could endure idleness; I began by digging up the potatoes and planting the winter crops, and in about a fortnight I had got it all in decent order; but on every finger was a mass of blisters, for not having handled fork or spade for nine years the flesh had become tender; however, as I had assisted my father, a blistered hand was of little consequence.

I had now spent three weeks in my old home, my native air having benefitted me very much, and as my health was greatly improved in every way, I made up my mind to look out for another situation. During this stay with my parents, I spent a very happy time among my old companions, at least, with those that remained, for many of them had left home like myself; two or three had gone to distant lands to seek a new home, never to return again. My old friend the owl still remained, however, and I did not forget my promise, for on the second night after my return, I took my usual walk up to the old stile I have mentioned before, thinking I should receive a hearty welcome as on a previous occasion—my anticipations, however, were not realised, for no sound did I hear; I tried again the next night but with the same result; I began to think some ruthless hand had levelled a gun and taken away the life of my bird, but on the third visit being somewhat later at night, I had the satisfaction of again hearing the old note, which resembles the syllables, hoo-hoo-hoo; here, then, was a welcome for me after an absence of three years, and could his cordial greeting have been translated, it might have been rendered "should auld acquaintance be forgot." During the short time I remained at home I paid a nightly visit to him and was always rewarded. But how true the old saying, "The best of friends must part," as I and the old owl did; but if he is still in existence, I wish him well, and that he may long enjoy a quiet home in his hollow tree.

I now began to make enquiries about another situation, and in a few days I was informed that a Mr. Bowley, one of the managers of the County of Gloucester Bank, in Cheltenham, was in want of a man-servant; I immediately applied for the post and was successful in obtaining it, and everything was satisfactorily arranged with the exception of my character, which I ventured to think was all right. My anticipation proved correct, for in a few days Mr. Bowley received, what was to me, a pleasing report concerning me, and it was arranged for me to go to him in a week from that date. I therefore commenced making preparations for another start, my dear mother overhauling everything I possessed, in order that my outfit might be rendered presentable. This proved to be the last time that I was to have a loving mother's care and attention bestowed upon me, as will be gathered from the next chapter.

CHAPTER IX.

My Arrival in Cheltenham.

HAVING now attained the age at which all young men feel proud, that of twenty-one, and having, during the last eight years, come in contact with many of my superiors, I felt myself "someone," as may be supposed. All my luggage being ready, I was prepared to take my departure. I therefore made a call upon my old friends and companions, just to say good-bye, and the next morning at nine o'clock I turned my back once more upon all that was dear to me. I took coach again at Perrott's Brook for Cheltenham, and went direct to my new situation, No. 22 Suffolk Square. The family consisted of master, mistress, and three children. I was somewhat unsettled for several days, but as time went on and the new faces seemed to grow old, I felt I was no longer a stranger, I found both master and mistress very agreeable, kind and considerate to all of us, but most particular in everything, not that the latter characteristic is objectionable, for a particular employer makes a particular servant. In the early part of the second summer I was with them, they arranged to go to the Isle of Wight for a change. Now this was most agreeable news to me, I having to accompany them. Accordingly, at the end of a week, we set off, our route being via Swindon, Reading and Basingstoke, crossing the Channel to Ryde. This being the first time I was ever on the water, I soon felt the effects of it, and as the steamer began to rise and plunge, I thought we were all going to the bottom of the sea. A kind of hurricane arose which added to the roughness of the water. By the way, there always is a storm when a landsman makes his first voyage, and generally of such a kind as to alarm even the captain; why is it? I was quickly ordered below, and no sooner did I get there than I felt I must go above again. Oh! dear, I shall never forget the feeling— truly horrible! I quite thought I was dying, and never wish to experience the like again. When lying more dead than alive, my thoughts wandered back to dear home; oh! how I longed to be there again in the old chimney corner, where I could have reclined my troubled head in the bosom of a mother!

Perhaps, though, this would not have been the kindest way of showing affection for her. On arriving at the landing stage, my first duty was to look after the luggage, but I felt I was of but little use, and a fellow servant kindly undertook that responsibility for me, for I was quite unable to see to anything. We at once drove to an hotel where tea was soon provided, and after partaking of a cup I felt a little better; but, oh! the motion of the boat all night was something terrible! I seemed to feel I was still on it, and quite a fortnight elapsed before I recovered from the horrid sea sickness. I feel sure that what I endured at that time will prevent me from ever emigrating to a distant part of the world, for I should never reach there alive. During our stay I enjoyed myself very much, rising early every morning to take a walk on the beach there to collect shells and the many different coloured sea-weeds,—specimens of the latter I preserved in many ways, and some of them are now hanging in my rooms as mementoes of the year when collected. I spent a little time in bathing every day, and the weather then being very hot the luxury was most enjoyable, but I had to pay dearly for it, as will presently be seen. We had spent about seven weeks there, when it was arranged for us to return to Cheltenam the following week. Three days before our leaving, I was seized with a most violent head-ache, which continued for two days and nights, and the second night fever set in, and gradually increased; in fact, I was delirious at times. A medical man was sent for, who at once pronounced it a case of bilious fever, brought on from over-bathing. Of course I was confined to my bed, and there I was, a prisoner—very much against my will, as may be supposed. My master and mistress returned home, leaving me behind in the care of the good woman of the house, and the doctor, who both paid me every attention; and through the skill of the latter, I was able to leave my bed in about ten days. At the end of three weeks I began to feel myself again, and on consulting my adviser, he said I might undertake the journey home with safety, and as soon as I pleased. I was not long in packing up, and glad I was to get off towards home once more; but all pleasant thoughts of the return seemed crushed when I first stepped on the boat, the same one that had brought me over a few weeks before. Knowing what I endured then, the very sight of the dark water seemed to chill me with horror; however, I bore up wonderfully, and the sea being very calm I did not feel the sickness as I expected I should, although I felt the motion of the boat for several days after. On reaching Swindon, I began to feel very hungry as I did some years before when the old pig stole my dinner; I therefore had a cup of tea with one small slice of bread and butter for which, I remember, I paid sixpence I considered this extortionate, and although I have passed through the station many times since, I have never left any more of my money there, and I dont think it likely I ever shall. The ten minutes allowed for refreshment having expired, I continued my journey, arriving in Cheltenham about half-past six, and made my way to my situation, where all seemed as glad to see me again as I was to see them. I cannot speak too highly of the kindness shown me by my master and mistress who did all they could to hasten my recovery. A meal was prepared for me, and then I was ordered to bed; I slept soundly for two or three hours, when I began to get very restless and in a dream; I fancied I was on the steamer again and heard the captain calling out, "Stop her, ease her," then I fancied I was leaning over the side looking at the rolling waves when they suddenly dashed over the deck. I awoke with a start and found my head had slipped off the pillow and was hanging over the side of the bed. I certainly enjoyed a laugh, at myself. The next day I resumed my work, going on as usual, and gathering strength every day I soon found myself quite well again and fit for anything. I thought it rather singular, however, that as soon as I began to mend, my hair began to fall off, but this, I learnt, was owing to the fever I had been suffering from.

For two or three years I had felt rather unsettled in my mind as to continuing in domestic service; I had a wish to get some situation on the railway— and thought I should like a guard's post.—I, therefore, mentioned the matter to my master, who said he did not wish to part with me as I suited him very well; but if I really wished to go, he promised he would use his influence in my behalf, and being one of the Directors of the Great Western Railway, he thought he could soon get me on. He at once communicated with the proper authorities relative to the matter, and in a few days I was sent for to Gloucester to see the District Manager previous to going to London. Oh! how all my hopes seemed raised at once! I pictured myself already in harness, with the blue frock coat, cap with gold band, and whistle slung to a button-hole; I fancied I could see myself shutting the doors of the carriages, calling out at the top of my voice, "Any more going on?" But how vain were my anticipations, and how often are such nipped in the bud. My bright visions of the future were quickly and rudely dispelled, for on presenting myself before the Superintendent the next day, I underwent a short examination as to character, and length of time in service, and subsequently was ordered on to the measuring stand to test my height—I am not usually nervous, but, Oh! how I shook, my knees literally bending under me—however, I pulled myself together as well as I was able and stretched every sinew in my body, for I knew the critical moment had come, in fact, I was almost standing on my toes, when I was told to stand with my feet quite flat; I then gave one last and final strain, but all to no purpose, I heard the judge say, "One inch and a half too short," this announcement settled the whole thing. At that time, I think, I must have been about five feet eight-and-a-half inches, and the required height, I believe, was five feet ten inches. All my plans being thus frustrated, and ending in nothing as it were, I made up my mind to go on as I had been going a little while longer, and think no more of the steam engine; but up to the present day I have always felt I should have liked the post. A few weeks after this little event, a new inmate was introduced into the household—a very genteel looking young person, her age about twenty.—The morning she arrived I happened to open the door to her, there she was, in a cab, with her luggage; of course I handed her out, and as I did so I said to myself, what a nice looking young woman, how neatly she is dressed, how clean she looks! Now, my readers, may perhaps, wonder why I am so particular in describing this lady, but the secret is, she subsequently became my wife. I remained in this situation about the same period I had done in each of the former ones, three years, and having by this time managed to save nearly one hundred pounds, I regarded myself as a rich man—and this amount I had deposited in the

Savings Bank, at Cirencester, where it had gained a little interest. Considering this sum a nice little nest egg, and having obtained consent of the lady to whom I have referred, to become Mrs. White, I mentioned the subject of my intended marriage to my master and mistress, who certainly were a little surprised; notwithstanding this, they received the information very cordially, and entertained the matter in a most unselfish manner. Having made them acquainted with my intentions, I gave the usual notice once more to leave in a month; and during the few weeks I had to remain all went on as usual, the general topic of the house during that period, being my forthcoming marriage. Once again did I make preparations for a new departure, but this time I did so with more pleasure than on leaving either of my former situations. Both, master and mistress, were anxious to know what I was going to do when married; but as I intended doing so many things, I could not well give a precise answer. My master, however, told me if he could be of service to me at any time, he would assist me most willingly; for during the three years I had been with him I had given him great satisfaction; and that he was, therefore, prepared to give me a good character. I little thought then I should require his recommendation in so short a time afterwards, as proved to be the case, but of this I shall speak in the next chapter. My notice having expired, I once more bade adieu, leaving the home of others, to enter one that was destined to become my own.

CHAPTER X.

Married.

ANIMATED by new thoughts and feelings of a more serious and sombre hue than those which had hitherto moved me, I grew somewhat timorous as to the future, but I took for my motto, "Hope on, hope ever." On leaving my situation in Suffolk Square I immediately made for Cirencester for the purpose of consulting a very old friend of my dear mother's,—a Scotchman,—a tea dealer, who had supplied her with tea for many years. I had come to the conclusion that there was plenty of room in Cheltenham for a business of the same kind, and so felt inclined to make a start as he had done, for he had succeeded in forming a good connection. His wares consisted of tea and coffee, and his practice was, to call on his customers once a fortnight.—On laying my plans before him, he very kindly offered to assist me in every way he could, and also proposed to take me in his shop for a month free of charge. He suggested initiating me into all the trade secrets connected with the articles I should have to dispose of ; the mixing and weighing, also the purchasing of the goods in their various stages of growth. I gladly accepted his offer During the time I was with him I was not idle, for I made the best use of my eyes, as well as hands, in diving into the pith of everything, for I seemed to see a large field before me where work might be done and progress made. I busied myself day by day in helping him all I could in his shop, not being particular as to what I did, first mixing the tea and coffee, numbering the different kinds in their order, and serving the customers, all of which I presumed would be to my advantage on commencing business for myself. At the end of the month my adviser considered I was quite competent to manage for myself. He certainly acted towards me as a true friend, and rendered me services which I have never forgotten; but he said he had done what he had out of regard for my mother, whom he highly esteemed; and like that mother he has gone to his rest.

I was somewhat at a loss to find a suitable place to carry on my business, but I found some rooms at No. 8 Victoria Street,

Fairview, Cheltenham, which answered every purpose; this, then, was the mansion for the new settlers. The first thing to be done was to lay in a stock of goods, which I did, purchasing them from my adviser in Cirencester. I was then ready for action, and having made all comfortable, I gave my future partner an invitation to come and judge for herself, which she did, expressing her entire satisfaction with my domestic arrangements. We, at the same time, settled that the event which should give her the right to superintend my household should take place on Wednesday the 23rd day of March, 1847, at St. Mary's, the Old Parish Church of Cheltenham. The service was performed by the Rev. T. P. Boultbee, then Curate of the Church, and later on Theological Tutor of Cheltenham College, when he took the afternoon service at St. Luke's, for there being, then, no chapel attached to the College, the Collegians attended this latter Church twice every Sunday, morning and afternoon.—The happy event being over, I at once set to work in right good earnest, soliciting every person I knew in Cheltenham, to whom I introduced my tea and coffee. The first day I went out I disposed of about twenty pounds' weight, which was far beyond my expectations; the second day, thirteen pounds; the third, ten pounds. This I looked upon as a grand success, and it certainly gave me great encouragement. I arranged to call on my customers once a week, which I did most punctually, never missing one. I generally left home with my bag of goods at nine in the morning, getting through my day's work by three or four in the afternoon; and by that time I was quite ready for my dinner, or rather early tea, having taken nothing since breakfast, except a sandwich prepared and carefully wrapped up by my new housekeeper. How sweet was it then, to sit down with her and talk over all the events of the day, while the tea and toast were fast disappearing. Ah! this was a pleasant time indeed, for both, the sun shining all round us; we, then, little thought there was a storm gathering in the distance. I continued my work daily, meeting with new customers in all directions; and at the end of the week, found myself in receipt of a very fair profit, averaging from twenty to twenty-five shillings. True, I had to walk a good many miles for it, but this I quite enjoyed: therefore, the toil became light.

I continued this work for some months, but finding I had more spare time on my hands than I cared for; and that my customers were increasing, I deemed it advisable to take a small shop, where I could increase my stock of goods. On mentioning the subject to my young wife, and asking her opinion, she said "You had better not venture, as you are doing pretty well now,—but do as you like, I will not advise you in any way, in case you should do wrong—but I don't think I would risk it." Had I taken her advice, I should not have lost the few pounds I was worth, as subsequently proved to be the case. I found there would be a shop to let in a few weeks, close to where we were living; the then occupant, a grocer, being desirous of giving up the same owing to failing health, I at once saw the owner, to whom I had been known for several years, and he accepted me forthwith as tenant. I soon made arrangements with the occupier, in taking to most of his stock, which was not very heavy, also the fixtures. A few alterations having been made by the landlord, and the general stock added to, I became sole proprietor of the noted grocer's shop, in Victoria-street,—what a position for one to occupy!—but far better would it have been for me, had I never ventured upon the scheme from which my wife endeavoured to dissuade me.—I had now become a general dealer, and having laid out the whole of my little capital in the purchase of goods, my shop presented a very respectable appearance. Here, then, was the country boy, who a few years previously had been taking care of his master's swine, but now was sole manager of the Victoria stores! Certainly, this was progress; and although the business had been neglected for some time, I soon saw it was not too late to work it up again—I was determined that nothing should be wanting on my part to ensure success.—I, therefore, threw the whole of my time and energy into the work; and in a few weeks had the satisfaction of seeing a trade was to be done. I now felt I was on the right road to make my way in the world, and I went on working and hoping for about six months. On going over my books, and balancing my accounts at the end of this period, I was startled to find the balance on the wrong side. However, I pushed on all I could, rising early every morning to clean and set the shop in order, as on four days in the week I had to call on my outlying customers, each journey occupying about seven or eight hours. During my absence, my wife had to look after the shop, which she certainly managed very well; she was doing her best at home, while I was exerting myself out, calling anywhere and everywhere. We both worked very hard—doing all we could for an honest living—and we found the custom gradually increase, week by week.

At the end of the first year, however, I was grieved to find I had so many names on my book, which ought not to have been there, and that some of the items were rather heavy; I had gone on and on, trusting many, until I found I was getting short of cash, which was a great difficulty; for I had constantly to replenish my stock of sundries to keep the shop going, and I found that my hundred pounds were nearly exhausted. I still struggled on against it all, doing the best I could for another six months, but I then saw it would be impossible for me to keep on the business; I had had numerous losses, having met with several dishonest customers who had taken advantage of me. It was then I found I was unable to pay my creditors their last account; true, they were not many, only three, their claims altogether amounting to about forty-five pounds, and my books showed in debts about fifty-five in my favour. My first step was to get an interview with each of the persons I was indebted to, explaining my true position, and offering to give over to them the whole of my stock-in-trade;

but this they refused to accept, being satisfied as to the way my business had been carried on; they only asked me one question as to "What I intended doing?" and upon my answering them to their satisfaction, each one said, "Pay me when you can!" This I considered very kind and generous of them, and they all expressed a great deal of sympathy with me, and bade me hope for the best—this greatly cheered me it is true—but sympathy, be it ever so great, does not entirely heal nor free the burden. After giving the matter mature consideration, I saw there was nothing to be done but to clear out of the shop in the best way I could, which I did accordingly; disposing of all that was left—a little to one, and little to another until the whole had gone.—In about ten days, my little shop which had been well stocked with an assortment of goods for the convenience of the public had passed away, and all my hopes for the future had gone with it. Here, then, stood the boy again, his hundred pounds had taken wings! flown away! Here he was, but not alone, for he had a sympathising wife, willing to lighten his load all she could; and besides, there was a baby-boy who had been born to us, and who was then some six months old. A person living near me, a well-to-do man, or as he was termed, a "gentleman," came to me, saying "He was very sorry I was in such difficulties; and after learning from me how I stood, suggested to me the practibility of altering the figures and entries in my books of account, and putting down an extra hundred pounds in my favour, making my bad debts appear so much the more, and then file my petition and pass through the Bankruptcy Court." Here was advice for me, for one, who had never been guilty of even the smallest act of dishonesty. Here, was it coolly suggested, that I should degrade myself by perpetrating an infamous fraud. I shall never forget the feeling that came over me on hearing his words; but there seemed to be a voice speaking within me, saying, "Will you dishonour that loving father and mother, who cradled you, nursed you, watched over you, and tended you when a babe; no, no, be honest in all your dealings, and you will overcome every trial." All this rushed through my mind in less time than it has taken me to write it. My reply was, "I am very much obliged to you, sir, for the advice you have given me, but I cannot act upon it; I will let the worst come, I will sooner starve than be dishonest, I am able to work, I have to support a wife and child, and I feel sure I shall never do it by acts of fraud; no, I will walk through the streets of Cheltenham an honest man." I was determined that it should not be said of me—

> "Lives of loose men still remind us,
> We can go the pace that kills,
> And departing, leave behind us
> Nothing but a lot of bills."

He then made an offer to collect my debts for a commission at the rate of ten per cent., which offer I unfortunately accepted, as will shortly be seen. Looking over my books, he calculated it would take him about six weeks to look it all up. I thought it was the best thing I could do under the circumstances, but I might have known that one who could suggest a dishonest act would himself be capable of committing it. At any rate I gave up my books to him, thinking it was all right, and at once began to look forward for a winding-up, so as to be in a position to pay my creditors and have a few golden sovereigns in my pocket again.

Alas! how soon bright hopes are crushed, as were mine; but at that time there was much comfort on the hope held out to me, and, indeed, it was all I had then to rest upon, for means, I had none, as may be imagined. I very anxiously looked forward for the time to come, when my supposed friend would have finished his work, receiving in return his commission; but all my expectations were in vain, and I was doomed to experience what, to me, was well nigh a crushing disappointment and disaster. My position was now most critical indeed. From my boyhood I had constantly struggled onwards and upwards, and I rejoiced in the pleasing thought—and it was accompanied with a profound feeling of thankfulness— that my endeavours to better my position had been fraught with success. Each step that I had taken upon the ladder of life had served to carry me higher, so high, indeed, that I almost fancied that my hand would touch the topmost round; but, alas! my self assurance now received a cruel and bitter blow, and I had to learn the lesson of old, that "All is vanity and vexation of spirit." My pecuniary resources were exhausted, my energy daunted, and hopes well nigh gone; yet was it absolutely necessary that I should once more begin life's battle, and that speedily, for I now had others dependent upon me. My thoughts for the future flew fast and furious, for all was going out, and nothing coming in; even the every-day commodities of life were rapidly increasing in price.

CHAPTER XI.

Man's Worst Enemy is Man.

BREAD at that time was one shilling the loaf, and potatoes three shillings and sixpence per peck,— the long to be remembered potatoe famine,— consequent upon disease having just commenced. I consulted my wife as to what steps I had better take in my unfortunate circumstances, and as she concurred in the idea that I had better take a private situation again, I accordingly began to make enquiries, mentioning it to every one I knew. In the course of a few days, a messenger came to me from the Gloucester Bank, saying a gentleman wished to see me at once. This was good news to me, and in a few minutes I presented myself before him. He informed me that a General Greenstreet, living at Ravensworth Lodge, on the Thirlestaine Road, Cheltenham, was in want of a butler, and he thought I should suit him. I lost no time in going to see the General, and, to my surprise, found he had already had an interview with Mr. Bowley, my last master. He had obtained all particulars from him as to my character, and was quite willing to engage me at once, providing we could make the necessary arrangements. The gentleman who sent for me had heard of my misfortune in business, and that I was looking out for another situation. He, therefore, communicated with the General at once, who expressed a wish to see me, so that the matter was almost settled between them. Fortunately, for me, my interview with the General resulted in my being engaged by him, it being arranged that I should enter his service at the expiration of three days, so as to allow me time to look for a suitable cottage for my wife and child. I very soon found one, in the Bath Road, a nice easy walking distance from my situation, as I had to sleep at home. At the end of the three days I had completed all my arrangements as to the removal of furniture; wife and child were comfortably settled. I was now ready for work once more, or, rather, to begin life over again, which I did in right good earnest.—I therefore entered upon my new duties, although the work was old; what a change again for me, from that of standing behind the counter! This was in 1849. The first day I was there the General asked me if I was a punctual man, as, being a military gentleman himself, he expected punctuality throughout the house. I replied in the affirmative, and, here, I may say that during the five years I was with him, I was only late on one occasion. I went very comfortably on for the first month, when I received my first wages and was enabled to at once discharge a small portion of my indebtedness. I have omitted to mention that at the end of a fortnight after entering this situation, I called upon the person who was collecting my debts, to see how he was progressing, when his statement was most favourable: he said he had got in about thirty pounds, and desired me to call upon him that day three weeks, when he hoped to hand me the full amount. How cheering this was to me; but little did I think he was only a wolf in sheep's clothing. Oh! how anxiously I looked forward for the day when I should be in possession of a few pounds again, and able to say I was out of debt and a free man! What sweet anticipations of the future; but these were not to be realised. The three weeks having expired, I made my way to him, on the very morning—punctual as usual. On reaching the house, the first thing that attracted my notice was a large bill in each window, announcing "This house to be let." A lady who lived next door, seeing me, came out and asked if I wanted to see Mr. C———. Of course I said "Yes." "Well," she said, "he is this very day passing his last examination in Bristol Bankruptcy Court." Here was a blow for me; I stood as one paralysed; my power of speech seemed to have left me, and my flesh seemed frozen.

Although this occurred so many years ago, it is to me, at the present time, a living memory. My feelings will never be forgotten; I at once made my way home to communicate the sad occurrence to my wife, knowing I should meet with her sympathy, being the only one I could go to in my trouble. As soon as I reached home I sat down, for I really felt quite ill; then came the first question from my better half, "What is the matter with you;" my reply was, "Oh! nothing of any importance," that was all I could say, for I felt quite lost. It was some minutes before I recovered myself, when I explained all to her. Here, then, was a second thorn, for I was now robbed of all—yes, without a shilling—robbed by one in whom I trusted, fleeced by my fellow man. The thought of being in debt was dreadful to bear, and I had no means of escape; I knew it would take years to pay it off, a little at a time, which it did. I well remember lying down that night, suffering from a terrific headache, brought on by the events of the day. Sleep seemed to have gone from me; there I lay, turning and tossing, and wondering if the man who had wronged me, felt as I felt then; through him I had become poor. Well, I forgave him, as I sincerely trust he has been forgiven. Having become a domesticated man, I found there were many expenses attending housekeeping, rent and taxes being rather a large item, so that I should have but little to spare for my creditors at the end of each month; however, I managed to pay each one a little on the receipt of my wages, this being accomplished by my careful wife looking after the trifles, and thus we managed pretty well. I now began to think I could devise other means of adding grist to the mill as I had several hours in the day of spare time, which I might turn to some account; and always being an early riser I had several hours in the morning, not being due in my situation until 7-30. I therefore learnt the French polishing, and soon becoming master of the art, I was enabled to add somewhat to my income. During the time I was in this situation, I was in the habit of rising very early in the morning; many times have I been on the top of Leckhampton Hill at half-past three, procuring specimens of birds, some of which may now be seen in my collection; and, although preserved nearly forty years ago, are still looking quite fresh, and in another forty will still be in as good a condition as now, unless, indeed, any unforeseen accident should befall them. I shall have passed away, but these cased songsters will still be there — mementoes of those early morning walks – collected, preserved, and mounted by my own hands, together with several cases of insects of various kinds, on which I have spent many hours of time in arranging and setting up, an occupation which always delighted me. It was at this time I began to have such a love for natural history in all its many branches. It is in the early spring and summer mornings the young Naturalist finds so many opportunities to pursue such a delightful occupation; for every step he takes, something is sure to attract his attention, the reposing butterfly, the active moth, the ever busy beetle, the crawling larve, seeking some quiet corner where to spin its silky cocoon and lay up during the time of its undergoing the great change, the extraordinary transformation season, which all insects undergo; when, from the disagreeable hairy caterpillar we often see in our walks, a beautiful painted butterfly comes forth from its entombed cell, possessing all the colours of the bright rainbow. What a beautiful type of man is all this! what a lesson one may learn from it! Again, in the early quiet morning when nature is wrapped in its dewy mantle, and the trees are just putting forth their green silky leaves, does it not bring out and set before us the great change that we must all undergo. The same again in the autumn of the year, when those green leaves assume a different tint and something seems to tell us that we, too, shall have our autumn, that we shall fade, wither, fall, and die, and, like the insect, shall undergo a great change, and then a beautiful spring. Oh! how much is all this for the thinking mind to dwell upon!—During the spring and summer months I was in the habit for many years of rising with the sun, first at seven o'clock, then at six, and often at three, spending three or four hours in my favourite pursuit before commencing my ordinary day's work. It was at this time I first entertained the idea of learning the bird stuffing. I thought perhaps at some future period of time I should find it useful, and that I might turn it to some profitable account, which I have done, inasmuch as it has, for several years past, formed my principal source of income. I well remember the first specimen I set up, being a robin. and very proud I felt when it was done; so I went on, filling up every minute of spare time I had, feeling determined to become master of the art by self perseverance. I would here mention that the only thing I ever saw done in connection with the business, was one small bird, skinned, from which I was able to gather a great deal. I then became acquainted with a gentleman who had acquired a good deal of knowledge in ornithology and from whom I obtained many hints which I have found most useful since.

How true the old saying, "One is never too old to learn;" for after preparing and setting up 6,049 specimens, as I have done up to the time of writing, I still find I can learn, and that there are many little touches and finishing strokes that may be given to the work, never thought of or introduced before. The largest specimen I ever set up was a fox, the smallest a flea, and this latter was a British one, a very fine one, being an adult specimen, and may still be seen in my collection. I remained with the family I have named for five years, all going on most comfortably in every respect, my own built canoe sailing along on the smooth waters with all sails unfurled, not a ripple to impede its progress. The lease of the house having run out, the family decided not to renew it, but settled upon going to a little village named Frenchay, near Bristol; both master and mistress asked me to go with them, not wishing me to leave them, but this I most respectfully declined doing, not wishing to leave Cheltenham. I will here mention in passing that during the time I was with them a Colonel Hancock, a brother officer of the General, they having served together in India, was in the habit of calling upon him, also a son, the Rev. Fraser Hancock, of whom I shall have to speak later on, as he became Vicar of St. Luke's Church, the Sunday services, at that time, being carried on by him in the present national school, previous to St. Luke's Church being built. All was soon settled for the break up, furniture packed up, and soon on its way for Frenchay, and I was again thrown upon my own resources. Happily, however, during the five years I had been in this, my last situation, I had managed to pay my creditors, for on receipt of my last quarter's wages, I paid the last instalment of my debts, and I stood once again a free man. By constant toiling, working, scheming, and planning, I had achieved what I looked upon as a great work, for I had been enabled to pay off all my liabilities, and to come out of the whole thing with clean hands. But what a period of anxiety had those five years been to me; what pain and wretchedness did I experience during those long years, and all through the dishonesty of one man. Only those who have passed through such an ordeal can in any way realise the sorrow it occasions. To the end of my life shall I remember the day I made the last payment and cleared off the whole debt. Oh, what a relief to my mind; I was as one who had been imprisoned for years, and then let free to enjoy all the beauties of creation once more!

I was now again out of harness, and uncertain what I should attempt next.

Money, I had none, but was in the enjoyment of good health, plenty of energy, and able to work, which I considered a great boon. Had I been alone I really think I should have tried my luck in some other country, notwithstanding my horror of the sea, but my wife and child were entitled to my first thoughts and consideration.—I had been at home two days, which I spent in putting straight the garden attached to our little cottage, when a friend of mine called upon me to tell me of a situation likely to suit me, with a lady in the promenade. I very soon made off and obtained an interview with her, and, on hearing where I had been living, she at once engaged me, subject to my character proving satisfactory, but I knew this would be no obstacle On the fourth day I received a very polite note, saying my testimonial was to hand from my good old master, and highly satisfactory in every way. My new situation was represented to me as a first-class one, the ladies, three in number, being particularly quiet and seldom going out to any late parties. The first week I was there, however, I found it somewhat different, for three nights out of the six I had but little sleep, having to fetch them at all hours, and I took a dislike to my engagement at once; I felt I could never adapt myself to it, but I managed to get through six months, when things reached a climax. One very cold night, the ladies had gone to a late party, and I was ordered to go for them at a certain hour and send in to let them know I was there with the fly. Punctual to the time I was there, asking the waiter who opened the door to please tell them at once, but I don't believe he did, for after waiting upwards of an hour, my mistress came out herself, asking if I was there. I answered "Yes, I have been here waiting a long time and almost frozen." Perhaps my reply was a little too abrupt; at any rate it gave offence, for the next morning after removing the breakfast the subject was mentioned to me, and was looked upon as one of a very serious nature. I threw the whole blame upon the waiter for not announcing my arrival at the time. However, she said it was a matter she could not possibly look over, and thought I had better leave her service. I thought so, too, and embraced the opportunity to express my disappointment in the situation, having found it very different from what I had anticipated, and I received a month's notice, which I very readily accepted. This was the sixth situation I had taken since I left my father's home, but the first time I had given any offence; and even this was not of a very serious character, grave as it was represented to me to be. I began now to think seriously of my position, and confess I was very unsettled in my mind as to what I should do, for I didn't seem to like the idea of taking another private situation. A few mornings afterwards I accidentally met an old friend in the Bath Road, who, on hearing I was leaving my situation, asked me if I should like a lodging house, thinking I was a likely man to get on in one. My reply was, "Yes, indeed, I should, the very thing I have been thinking about," but added, that having no capital, I feared I should have to abandon the idea. My friend said, "Well, there is a house to let in Rodney Terrace which will just suit you; meet 'me to morrow morning at eleven o'clock, and in the meantime I will see what can be done." In the morning I met my friend at 13, Rodney Terrace, and with him proceeded to look over the house. I saw at once it could be divided into two suites of apartments with sufficient accommodation for ourselves. But I placed before him my position, and stated that I did not well see how I could commence. "Oh," he said, "I will put you in the way how to manage, for I have already consulted a friend upon the matter, who is now waiting to see you." So we set off at once to see a worthy house furnisher, to whom, as it appeared, I was very well known, and he accordingly said he was prepared to furnish my house and make the terms of payment easy for me. My next step was to see the owner of the house, not feeling sure he would accept me as a tenant; we therefore paid him a visit when he very readily accepted me as a yearly tenant, and I then gave my final orders as to furnishing the house, and that it was to be ready in three weeks from that date. The time having expired for me to leave my situation, I once more collected my belongings and took my leave, on the 24th of April, 1853. This was the winding-up of my private service, and the day I left was a kind of holiday to me. I would just mention that I took my departure on very good terms, but I felt very glad to get away, especially as my head was so full of the new undertaking. The next morning I set to work, making preparations, for I was determined not to remain idle very long. The first thought was to get someone to take my cottage, having it on my hands for another six months, and in a few days I succeeded in finding a respectable man who took it at once. This being settled, we had nothing to do but to "move," which feat we successfully accomplished within the next day or two. It was with no slight feeling of regret that I left the cottage, for we had resided there for five years and six months, and during that time I had made several improvements in the little garden, such as forming a fantastic rockery—many of the stones I carried from Leckhampton Hill, very early in the spring and summer mornings—a nice little bower of creeping clematis, and a sweet scented jessamine overhung the portals of the doorway. But all has been changed, nothing left, save the clinging, green ivy, towering to the topmost storey of the adjoining shop; this same ivy having been planted by me in little slips, in the year 1851. As I look at it now when I pass, many old associations are revived, and I live over again the times and scenes of long ago.

For the first two or three days, it is needless to say, we were all fully occupied in setting our new abode in order and rendering it fit to receive, as we hoped, the guests who were speedily to arrive. It was with many a qualm and fear that we proceeded with our work, for the thought very naturally arose that our new venture might not be a successful one. Our fears, however, were greatly allayed, for at an early date, through the kind recommendation of a friend, we had the pleasure of securing a tenant for one suite of apartments for three months. At the end of this period, to my very great delight, certain relations of the gentleman who had become our tenant joined him at our house, the whole of which they took for the succeeding twelve months. With this certainty before me, my prospects for the future grew somewhat brighter, and I began to indulge the hope that ere long I should be enabled to discharge my obligations to my friend the house furnisher. Having by this time grown accustomed to my new mode of life and its many requirements, I found I had vacant time to spare during the day, which might be profitably occupied. Many were the services, therefore, that I rendered my friends and neighbours, services of no great importance in themselves, but of sufficient value to be paid for, and I was thus enabled to add to my income to no small extent.

It was at this period that I first donned the "swallow tail" and white tie that decorate the individual, who, from once occupying a position that called forth the (perhaps merited) satire of a Dickens, has now become a public necessity. I allude to the "itinerant waiter." For thirty-four years have I adopted this calling, more or less, and during that period have been successful in securing a very fair share of the work in and around Cheltenham. My experience during that period has, of course, been extensive and varied, and has embraced incidents which compelled me to turn from "grave to gay, from lively to severe." Funeral, christening, ball, and wedding all came alike and in their turn to me. Writing of weddings, I am reminded that I have seen many happy couples starting upon their honeymoon, locked in railway carriages, especially at the Great Western Station, booked to various parts of the world, and generally by what is known as the "Bride's Train," the 1-55. There I have seen the happy pair over and over again, sitting side by side, difficult to say which looked the happiest. I could tell many little tales in connection with those happy gatherings, but should be straying away from the main point, which I have already done; but when standing behind the chair of the bride I have often felt amused on seeing her nudge her husband to get him on his feet to return thanks for the health which had just been proposed for himself and bride. I remember on one occasion the bridegroom was particularly bashful; turning round, he asked me if I would return thanks for him. Of course I couldn't do that; but I whispered in his ear, "You had better get up, sir, and just say a few words," which he did, hanging down his head and playing with his watch chain. He managed to glance round the table and say in stammering tones, "Thank you, my friends, for coming here to-day; it is very kind of you," the poor bride all the while blushing the deepest crimson. I am pleased to say the happy pair are still alive and residing in Cheltenham at the present time; and if this little work should chance to fall into their hands, they will doubtless remember the event I have here recorded.

As a waiter I should like to protest against the fashion of writing the bill-of-fare in French. If it were a decent language I should not object, for no doubt *faisan* possesses a better flavour than pheasant;

but when it allows of every waiter having a distinct (or indistinct) pronunciation of his own, and the guests still another, I think that such a language ought to be swept from the face of the earth and the dining table. I can quite see the necessity for calling dishes by foreign names, but would it not be simpler to use a tongue that everybody can understand, say Volapük? This fashion renders it essential for a waiter to learn French now-a-days, at least, French as given in *le menu d'un repas* (a different thing perhaps); and the acquisition of this language has given me many an aching head. It has also given aching sides to my listeners. But I believe I am now tolerably proficient and equal to any average *menu*. The only thing I stipulate for is that the guests stick to the card and take the dinner straight through from top to bottom, and don't jump from one course to another, otherwise the study of many years is entirely set at naught. For instance, a gentleman once said "Garçon" as I passed his chair; and when I replied "I don't think we have any, sir, is it on the card?" he and his fair companion were convulsed with laughter. All that I ask is stick to the *menu*, and no tricks. Still I must repeat that society has selected a bad language, for everybody knows, even Mark Twain says the French are all right, but they can't spell worth a cent.

I am now enabled to make a jump over a period of about eight years; for during this period the events that went to make up the sum of my and our everyday life, were such as to need no special chronicle. A constant round of care and anxious thought with here and there an occasional break, prevailed during the years to which I allude. One object I had only before me, and that was to retrieve my former position and win back from fickle Dame Fortune the favour she once bestowed and then took from me. Had I needed a special incentive to further my exertions, the same would have been afforded me by the numerous additions to my family during this period of eight years. We had then born to us a second son and two daughters. The former, a bright blue-eyed, fair-haired little fellow, died at an early age, just as he had grown useful to us and the world was opening out before him; the daughters have now blossomed, or, rather, bloomed into matronly women, with little ones of their own. As these infant voices fall from time to time upon my ear, I live over again the years that have flown and recall the first bright beam of "childhood sunshine," which fell across the threshold of our own cottage door.—Notwithstanding the many and increasing demands upon my income during these eight long weary years,

I was enabled, by rigid and continued perseverance and self-denial, to discharge my indebtedness to my friend, the house furnisher, and once more stood "monarch of all I surveyed."

At this period of my life I had so many irons in the fire that I was once more happily enabled to make provision for a rainy day.

Nearly the whole of the land in the immediate neighbourhood of St. Luke's Church was unbuilt upon, and certain freehold building plots, now known as "St. Luke's Terrace," being in the market, I determined to become a landed proprietor. Selecting what I considered to be the most favourable spot, I and the owner were enabled to strike a bargain, and I became possessed of a certain number of square yards of land that I could call, and were, in fact, my own. Satisfied with the one speculation, I next determined upon erecting for myself a house, so turning architect, I sketched the class and kind of building I desired. This done, I consulted a worthy builder, who is now no more, and terms being agreed upon, we jointly raised the dwelling house I and my family now inhabit, and which, having regard to the love I had ever cherished for the home of my youth, I not unnaturally christened "Bagendon House." Now that the row of houses, of which it forms part, is completed, it is otherwise known as "No. 2, St. Luke's Terrace." Many curious friends may be ready to exclaim, "How did you manage to do so much and so well?" To their kind enquiries I would reply " By perseverance, untiring energy, and self-denial;" and I may go a step further and confess that the legal conveyance of the land is in my own keeping. It must not be thought that my prosperity was entirely unclouded, far from it, for I had much to depress and dishearten me. In addition to the many troubles and petty annoyances that visit each and all of us day by day, we received a sad blow by the death of our second boy, and not long afterwards I myself was laid low by a severe illness, which nearly proved fatal. Thanks to a vigorous constitution, the careful nursing of my wife, and the kind and unremitting attention of my skilful attendant, Dr. Gabb, who will, I am sure, forgive me for thus publicly alluding to him, I recovered and was mercifully spared still "to labour and to wait."

As we went on from year to year, I did not forget my old home, Bagendon, for every now and then I paid a flying visit, setting off in the morning as early as four o'clock, and reaching there at eight, in time for breakfast; and certainly quite ready for it, after the walk of thirteen miles. I generally spent the day in roaming about the fields, and visiting the old spots so familiar, each scene seeming to speak of the past pleasures experienced. After the enjoyment of the day, I often walked home again in the evening. I well remember on one occasion doing so, and after walking about eight miles, I became foot sore, sitting down under a tree near Cowley, with the hope that some conveyance would come past, when I could get a "lift;" but in this I was disappointed. This was on a dark November night, so pulling myself together in the best way I could, I made a fresh start, having five miles before me. I had great difficulty in walking, as one of my feet had become terribly blistered: I therefore took my boots off, thinking, perhaps, I could travel better without them, but not being in the habit of going barefooted. the trial proved a failure. On reaching the top of Charlton Hill, and seeing the lights of dear old Cheltenham, they seemed to give me new energy, and I reached home about half-past ten, after one of the most painful walks I ever experienced, and ever to be remembered.

CHAPTER XII.

Sunny Days.

AT the end of the year 1852, the building of St. Luke's Church was commenced. A lady friend whom I had known some time, recommended me to try and obtain the office of verger, saying, she was sure I should stand a very good chance, and she promised to give me a good testimonial herself, and also see the

Rev. Fraser Handcock, being personally acquainted with him, as he was to be the vicar. This seemed to be a step in the right direction, and one which would probably advance me further in life. A few days afterwards I met him, when he told me he had seen the lady, and that he would bear me in mind, particularly as he had known me when I was living with General Greenstreet, one of his father's old Indian friends. Well, time went on until late in the year 1854, when I began to gather up the many recommendations that I had been busy collecting for several months. I solicited nearly every lady and gentleman whom I knew, telling them my mission. I had no difficulty in obtaining what I wanted, and about three months before the church was completed, I deposited all my papers with the Rev. Handcock. I am not quite sure about the exact number, but I think my testimonials numbered twenty-five or twenty-seven. Whether it was by reason of the quality or quantity, I cannot say, but the fact was that my credentials enabled me to secure the position I desired and which I now hold.

On Wednesday, the seventh day of November, 1854, St. Luke's Church was consecrated, the late Dean of Carlisle, the Rev. Francis Close, preached the first sermon.

My old and respected friend, the late Mr. John Bennett, was then appointed clerk, and he and I entered upon our duties on that day. Long were we associated together, but to-day as I write, I realize the painful fact that I am the only one left of those who were connected with the church at its opening. Thirty-four years have passed away since that time, and as I now sit in my pew, I can recognise only two faces of the many who were present on that memorable occasion. It is with no little pride that I note the fact that during those thirty-four years, taking all the services and meetings, I have never been absent from a Sunday service, except upon three occasions, when illness prevented me from attending to my duties. With all respect I can say that during the period I have mentioned, many amusing incidents occurred, but I will only speak of one, which was connected with a wedding The Rev. Fraser Handcock's brother was the officiating minister, and on giving the ring to the man with the request to put it on the fourth finger of the woman's hand, he deliberately placed it on his own, and seemed quite astonished when told he must put it on that of the woman. I certainly sympathised with the bride, for the deep crimson which dyed her cheeks told me of the annoyance she was experiencing.—The Rev. Handcock was vicar for seventeen years, and at the end of that time he exchanged livings with the late Rev. J. A. Aston, who ministered with us for twelve years, leaving for Deptford, London. Canon Money, our late respected vicar, was with us five years, the present vicar being the Rev. G. Despard.

CHAPTER XIII.

A Bad Speculation.

NOT satisfied with my previous exertions, I still entertained the idea of doing something more for the future, so that in my declining years I might enjoy the result of my labour. I had for some time been thinking about the subject of Life Assurance, having many times been solicited to embark in it by a Mr. Grier, of Montpellier Villas, he being the local agent for the then Wellington Assurance Society, of London. After a good deal of persuasion, I was induced to take out two policies, one for myself and one for my wife, for one hundred pounds each, the premiums being payable every six months, and an extra premium annually; the sums assured being payable at death, or at the age of 62, whichever first happened, and we were to participate in the profits with bonuses. Well would it have been for me had I never joined it, but placed my spare threepenny pieces in the Savings Bank. Believing all was right, I kept up my payments for the next thirteen years, the Society having in the meantime amalgamated with a kindred Society, named the European. At the end of the thirteen years, when sitting at breakfast one morning, a letter was handed to me from the Chief Office in London, announcing the failure of the Society, but calling upon me for another six months' premium, as, by paying that sum, I should become entitled to a share in the dividend, and asking me to send the amount within a week. Well, I did send it, but not without many a murmur and pang of regret at the thought that the savings of years were once again to be swept away. I had risen early and had late taken rest, and this was the result of all. Here, then, was another 'thorn—robbed of all again'; I quite thought I must have broken down under the load I had to carry, for my energy seemed quite gone. However, I bore up in the best way I could, feeling it was no use to sit down and fret over it, as that would not restore the sum I had lost. I therefore bestirred myself, trying to forget the recent calamity, painful as it was to bear. Some three months after the winding up of the affair, I was agreeably surprised on receiving a cheque for five pounds, arising from the first dividend; this, indeed, was some consolation, and to a certain extent the evil was thus somewhat lessened; but still, the wound which had been inflicted was only partially healed. In about four months after this piece of good luck, a second dividend took place, my share of it amounting to seven pounds, fifteen shillings. Here was another good stroke of fortune; and in a few months more, the third and final dividend was declared, when I received a further sum of seven pounds, making a total of nineteen pounds, fifteen shillings. This, then, was the result of my speculation with the Wellington and European Assurance Societies.

At this time I was working my way in Cheltenham pretty well, having a fair share of work, and I believe I am right in saying that since my first wedding I have had the management of over two-hundred and forty others, both in town and country. Many ladies and gentlemen, who were children thirty years ago, have I seen grow up from their infancy, and, in after years, have attended at their own marriages. How often have I taken those little ones some little delicacy into their nurseries after a dinner party in the evening. As an illustration of the fact, I had a hearty shake of the hand only a few weeks ago from a lady who had just returned from India, after being away for twelve years. I did not recognise her at first, but she soon made herself known to me as she recalled to my recollection the little tit-bits she received from my hands while she waited in the stairs. Oh, how pleased I was to see her! This is one among the many instances to which I have referred.—All was now going on cheerily and most satisfactorily in every way, my children all growing up, and my way being comparatively prosperous, when, unexpectedly and without a word of warning, I experienced a sad domestic affliction in the sudden illness of my dear wife, who has, I regret to say, been a great sufferer, and still continues an invalid. At this point, however, I must confess that my respected publisher informs me that he is running short of capital " I's," and that I must needs, therefore, draw this autobiography to a close.

CHAPTER XIV.

Final.

GOING back in memory to the age I was four years old, which I well remember, I have given a faint outline of my wanderings from then until now. From the memorable morning of the nankeen trousers scene, I have dotted down all that has taken place until the present time, when I am about to bring these memoirs to a close. I trust I have "nothing extenuated" and "naught set down in malice." I have, in my own unpretending way, striven to make truth read as strangely as fiction, and have endeavoured to interest those to whom I have the pleasure of being known. While employed from time to time in penning these rugged thoughts, I have derived considerable pleasure from the awakening of the memories of the past. I should be vain, indeed, were I to think that the lines now traced have, in themselves, any intrinsic merit. Rather let me express the hope that having personally earned the respect of the reader, he will not cast aside what I have written as utterly worthless, but will deign to peruse it to the end. But little remains for me to add, now that the idea with which I started is approaching its fulfilment. I feel that I have unconsciously grown old. True it is that my hair is not yet tinged with grey, that my step is yet well nigh as elastic, as of old, and that I can still cover four miles an hour without the aid of a stick. These are facts, yet, nevertheless, I feel that having regard to the number of events I have here set down and the period over which they have extended, I must be growing old. I cannot say I shall leave behind me footprints on the sands of time, but I venture to express the hope that my life has not been an entirely mis-spent one; my very business has been such as to expand the mind, enlarge the views of life, banish unbelief, and send the thoughts from "nature up to nature's God."

In my first and last Chapters, I have spoken of my "vernal vigour and autumnal green," the secret of which I have often been asked to reveal, and it may not be out of place to state, once for all, the resolutions I have religiously kept through life, and to the observance of which I attribute under God's blessing, the health and energy I still possess.

Early hours, temperance in all things, and always to have so much work on hand, that I hadn't a moment to devote to unnecessary care, these have been the golden rules of my life.

I should like to mention that I had a notion to introduce some original poems between the covers of this Book, which would have been specially written. But my first effort in this direction was received with such derision, that I thought it best to abandon the idea. This first effort was an "Apostrophe to the Moon." A subject popular with all poets—and the opening verse ran—

> Great Queen of Night, who sheds thy light
>   O'er all the sleeping city
> And beholds the sight of the man that's "tight"
>   Going home with plaintive ditty!

This they declared to be no poetry. They said that among its other failings, it was a union of the sublime and the ridiculous. I admitted that it was so in a sense, and stated it was done with a purpose. I thought the picture of the moon shining serenely upon the city, once the scene of busy life and restless activity, but now wrapped in slumber, was effectively contrasted with, and heightened by the figure of the "afflicted" straggler; in short, I interwove in one short verse the cold and classical with the realistic. That man seemed humanizing a severe ideal. (I believe that is how the critics talk, isn't it?) But the main object of the verse remains to be disclosed.

The man was singing a plaintive ditty, of course to the moon. It is quite beside the question to say the man probably saw two moons or that his song was doubtfully articulated, for that I wish the reader to take for granted because it accentuated my chief idea. There was the Immortal Queen of Night, calm, cold, and virtuous—radiant in all her purity—far above this wicked world, and there was the Man-mortal steeped in vice and drink, the basest of his kind, pouring out his soul of love to her, the unattainable, and for the moment striving to conquer his nature and the staggers—in a word, it was Vice bowing before Virtue! That one verse in my opinion, was a masterpiece in itself. However my friends could not be convinced (although I pleaded that if it was not "Browning" it was at least "Whiting") and so with other effusions that poem must be lost to posterity.

As a concluding item with reference to my vocation of taxidermist, I would record the fact that from the period of my first commencing the art of bird preserving until now, I have prepared and set up no less than 6,966 specimens, grouping them and making up 2,049 cases, to say nothing of skins and insects, etc., likewise to be numbered by their thousands.

And now, "Farewell, a long farewell!" but prior to bidding it I must tender my grateful thanks to my many kind supporters in and around Cheltenham. They have been and still are, I rejoice to say, numerous, and they have been good enough to extend to me considerable kindness, personal friendship, and may I be permitted to say esteem. To one and all do I say most heartily and sincerely, I thank you. May all happiness be yours.

www.ingramcontent.com/pod-product-compliance
Lightning Source LLC
Chambersburg PA
CBHW080437110426
42743CB00016B/3195